Adventures for the Soul

35 INSPIRATIONAL POEMS AND
THE STORIES BEHIND THEM BY

Natalie Sleeth

Hope Publishing Company
CAROL STREAM   IL   60188

Ron and Natalie Sleeth, 1983

5

Composing at the piano

Molly, Ron, Natalie and Tom, December 1979

Tom, attorney, Molly, teacher

6

Natalie with grandchildren Kelli and Michael

Foreword

Some years ago, following a dinner in the home of our good friends, Natalie and Ronald Sleeth, my wife and I listened to some arrangements Natalie had written for a faculty show when Ron was teaching at Vanderbilt University. The sounds were as delightful as they were distinctive. This was not the usual wedding of familiar tunes with clever texts which expose faculty concerns, complaints, etc. While these texts were clever, Natalie's arrangements of the music evidenced unusual ingenuity.

I was not surprised when Natalie came to my office some time later to discuss what music courses she might take for continuing education. Since she was not interested in any advanced degree which would involve core requirements, I listed several possibilities including my class in Advanced Choral Arranging and suggested that she enroll as an auditor, which she did one fall semester. Fortunately, the class was smaller than usual that semester, so it was possible for Natalie to have her arrangements heard and appraised even though she was an auditor. Many of the students had difficulty completing the arrangements on assigned dates, but not Natalie. She always had her arrangements ready and, I suspected, earlier than required. For the rest of the class, Natalie's arrangements were both exemplary and intimidating.

It was obvious to me and the class that Natalie had exceptional skills in arranging. It was additionally obvious to me that there was a vast reservoir of creativity being barely tapped by the sequence of arranging projects. I sensed that she was frustrated, but hoped that the class experience had stimulated her creativity beyond the specifics of each assignment. It was soon evident that Natalie was "moving on" or that, as Ron said later, "she had been unleashed." Her subsequent creative productivity as a composer met needs and expectations shared by a host of directors, with the "Jazz Gloria" serving as an introduction. Even more remarkable is the fact that Natalie wrote her own texts. Her love of language and the tone color of words is matched by her ability to articulate her philosophical and theological thoughts in strophes that are as appealing as they are engaging. What a combination of creative gifts, and what a responsible use of these gifts! As she has said, she hoped to educate, enlighten and enrich a wide variety of singers through her poetry which shared her beliefs, concerns, ideals and dreams. This book affirms both the love and the hope as manifested in her poetic lines.

Throughout literary history there are poems that seem to defy musical setting. Indeed, some poets do not want their strophes set to music since they believe their lines lose identity as a poem. Many poems seem to solicit a musical setting, while the weakness of others becomes magnified or sometimes obscured when set to music. In Natalie's creative efforts, words and music always appear to have a "Gemini" relationship. Will those who know

10

Natalie's compositions hear music when the words in this book are read?

While the meaning and impact of a text can often be heightened in a musical setting, readers will enjoy a new and different encounter with Natalie Sleeth as her lines of poetry are read rather than sung. There will be time for review and reflection when the words are freed from the onward pull of musical progression. All who know Natalie Sleeth as a musician will come to know her more personally when reading her words.

DR. LLOYD PFAUTSCH
Professor of Sacred Music and
Director of Choral Activities,
Meadows School of the Arts
Southern Methodist University
Dallas, Texas

Sharings

Part of knowing who you *are* is knowing who you are *not*, so before I share both myself and my music, let me clarify who I am *not*. First of all, I am not a Choir Director (and never have been). I once had a brief experience "trying that on for size" and I concluded that it definitely did not "fit"! Second, I am not a composer of children's music only, even though a few of my anthems do fall into that category. (The criterion for deciding this is the text, not how easily singable the music is!) Third, I cannot write "on cue" and so do not accept commissions. My "Muse" cannot be counted on to produce a valid piece on a given schedule so I never promise what I might not be able to deliver. Fourth, I am no "wunderkind" who began producing music at birth/puberty; rather, I "discovered myself" circa age forty and have been composing ever since. Last, I do not compose religious music only, but occasionally (and happily) deal, also, with the secular world and write songs which are usable in schools and non-sacred situations. So—now that I have corrected several possible misconceptions, let me get on with who I *am!*

Although I have a musical background, consisting of fifteen years of piano, three years of organ and at least twenty-five years of singing in choirs and choruses of all sorts and descriptions, I never *planned* a career in music, never had a course in composition (though I majored in Music Theory in college) and did not think of myself as "creative" at all. It was only in the fall of 1968 that my life took an unexpected turn which led me into composition. My family had been in Germany for a year when my late husband (then a Professor at SMU in Dallas) had a sabbatical leave, and after we returned to Dallas in the late summer of '68, I found myself wondering what to do with my time since the children were then eleven and fourteen, and didn't need me to be a full-time mother only. By being away a year I had gotten off everyone's volunteer lists, and I didn't tell them I was back, so I could avoid repeating past patterns in the future. But what to do instead?

I decided, ultimately, to take some courses at SMU—to "stretch my mind"—and I therefore enrolled as an auditor in two courses taught by Dr. Lloyd Pfautsch in the Choral Department. I had known Lloyd for some time, as he directed the Dallas Civic Chorus in which I sang, so he was very willing to allow me to "sit in" on his courses in Choral Conducting and Choral Arranging—which I did. In the latter course, the class (which was small) was given weekly assignments to arrange folksongs or hymns for various vocal combinations; and, although an auditor, I found myself doing these assignments, handing them in to be sung by the class and much enjoying the activity. Dr. Pfautsch encouraged me to go on with arranging after the course was over, but I soon discovered that I felt frustrated by the limitations of using someone *else's* materials (which I could not change). So I said to myself, in effect, (having no idea where it would lead): "Maybe I could write my *own*" (both words and music) and that was the beginning. Thus I started *composing* rather than arranging, and wrote both the words and music for several pieces in the next few months.

13

I showed these compositional efforts to Dr. Pfautsch and again, he was most encouraging, even offering to send several of them to publishers for me. Before long I received several contracts for publication which opened a whole new world to me that I had never expected to enter. A turning point came in 1970 when Carl Fischer, Inc. published my piece, "Jazz Gloria," because it was virtually "right time, right idea" for that particular number, since many churches were "opening up" and singing music other than "Gloomy Gothic" (as my friend, Dale Wood, calls it). Carl Fischer also published the anthem in a bright red cover which caught people's attention and the piece just "took off," becoming a best-seller very quickly. Several other prestigious publishing firms contacted me with requests to write them a "Jazz Gloria" and I suddenly had to come to terms with what I *could* and could *not* do!

In retrospect I realize that this was a time of soul-searching in which I worked out my philosophy about what I was doing and *why* I was doing it, and came to terms with both my limitations and abilities. The insights which I gained from that self-evaluation are still with me and continue to govern my creative life. The most important insight which emerged from looking inward was the realization that above all I must be *free:* free from obligations to others (taking commissions, e.g.) which would put my "Muse" under pressure to produce "this piece by that date," and also free to throw out what I don't like and to keep trying until I am satisfied. I ultimately defined my goals as wanting to write "something worth singing" (a decent melody unlike many of the alto parts I'd sung), and "something worth singing *about*" (words that carry a meaningful message). I felt very strongly that I had not planned this creativity and that it seemed like a "gift of grace"; therefore, I needed to use my new outlet in a responsible way. (Another thing I realized was that I was not writing music for the money, though of course some remuneration both legitimatizes my creative efforts and is helpful to receive.) In any case, the "self-study" I did at this time was very helpful and affected my whole outlook on what I do creatively.

People often ask me which I write first—the words or the music?—and with few exceptions, for me, it is the words. However, the *thought* must precede the writing of the text because unless I decide what I want to write about, I don't get started! It isn't a question of wanting to write a "Christmas piece," for example, because "Christmas" is a *category* and not a *concept*. Until I can focus on the concept I want to impart in the words, I cannot truly begin. It is a matter of giving the "oblong blur" a *form* and if I can finally isolate the "thesis" with which I want to work, the first step has been taken. Then comes the task of finding a way to state the idea in words and to build a "skeletal text" expressing the thought effectively. Sometimes the whole creative process breaks down here, for even though I know *what* I want to say, I cannot find a *way* to say it that is acceptable to me. Actually, my process is one of continuous trial-and-error, which is extremely frustrating when I get nowhere, and extremely elating when I stumble on to the right way to phrase the text. The piece *can* develop very rapidly after that point has been reached, though that is not always true and some efforts abort even after a "handle" has been found.

I work at the piano every morning, for I am a morning person and feel most creative at this time of day. However, just sitting at the piano does not insure that

15

anything worthwhile will happen. On the other hand, if I do *not* sit there and work, I *know* nothing will happen so I discipline myself to work most every day and that very *doing* often makes "sparks fly" and brings other ideas to mind. It always takes me a while, after I have been away from composing, to get back in the groove, but I realize that over the years this has been my pattern, so I keep at it and try not to get discouraged. I am a born optimist (my husband used to call me Norma Vincent Peale) and I feel that any morning has the potential of bringing forth a piece, so each day anew I am hopeful!

In creativity there is also the role of the subconscious to consider, and this cannot be minimized, although it is hard to describe or to control. I have found—not always, but sometimes—that when my subconscious is bombarded with data ("iron filings," if you will) it may surprisingly sort these bits and pieces into a meaningful idea when I least expect it. I cannot *count* on it to solve the problem, but occasionally it does, and I am *amazed* at what results.

When I give workshops or talks about my creativity, I use—as illustrations of the way pieces "happened" for me—three different quotes and three different musical examples which seem to express concretely *my* particular creative process. The first is a quote of Leonard Bernstein's about collecting "bits and pieces" of seemingly unrelated kinds, and having them unexpectedly relate to one another and produce an idea which brings forth a piece. I, too, collect bits and pieces from various sources (anywhere from the Reader's Digest to a church bulletin) and paste them into a notebook wherever there's room, producing a very helter-skelter/heterogenous assortment of stimuli. One day, during a "lean period," when I was searching for an idea, I was thumbing through this book and opened to a particular place which had an article on spirituals on the right-hand page with the song "Were You There" underlined. I like spirituals and so part of my brain was empathetically pondering the phrase "Were you there?" when I looked at the left-hand page opposite and saw something there which had to do with Christmas. The two ideas jumped the page and "connected" and I began thinking: "Were you there . . . at Christmas? Well, no, you weren't and neither was I, but *what if we had been???*" And very quickly the idea took shape with an AABA form (Were you there? Did you see? Did you hear? Did you know?) and I had a piece! (Were You There on That Christmas Night?)

Another quote that describes how a piece "happened" for me comes from Robert Frost who said that for him, a poem began with "a lump in the throat" (indicating a feeling level rather than a thought as the starting point). I once pondered trying to paraphrase that familiar passage from Ecclesiastes about "For everything there is a season" . . . [and to set it to music] but I never found a way—perhaps because I don't *like* all the ideas expressed in that passage (a time to hate, e.g.). So I tabled the thought and went on with other things. Sometime later, however, a close friend of ours in another city died after a long and very brave battle with cancer, and my husband was asked to help conduct his memorial service. I went along, too, and was moved by the courageous attitude of his wife (which he, too, had exhibited during his long struggle), so I wrote her a note reflecting this after we returned home. She soon answered and the opening words of her letter were: "There's a time to live and a time to die" . . . and I immediately knew that I must try again to set the Ecclesiastes passage and to dedicate the anthem to our friend "in memoriam." Very soon I succeeded in doing this by writing a piece entitled: "It's All in the Hands of God" with a thesis which ties together the Ecclesiastes material as well as stating something which I firmly believe. Incidentally, any text I write has to be consonant with my beliefs although it will not, hopefully, be merely a personal statement but rather, a universal one pointing to a greater truth which others can appreciate and appropriate as well.

The third quote about creativity which illustrates my process is mine: "Creativity is the imaginative use of the materials at hand." One severe winter in W. Va. I was attempting to write a songbook for use in the schools; I had finished several numbers and was wondering what to work on next. That winter was the worst one in 100 years, according to the newspapers, and as I went toward my study one morning to compose, I passed the breakfast room where the TV was forecasting *more* snow and *more* cold temperatures and I thought: "I've had it! I'm sick of this stuff!" Thinking those thoughts I went right to work on a song called "The Winter's a Drag Rag" which expressed all my frustrations and made me feel much better about everything! (Humor is a good healer and the "light approach" to what is a real problem situation can sometimes be most helpful!)

Even though I can pinpoint, with the foregoing quotes, the ways that pieces have sometimes happened for me, the "mystery" of the creative process remains just that—a mystery—and that is part of its excitement. One never knows whether something valid will happen today or not, but, being an optimist, I get up every morning and think that *this* might be the day when a really *good* idea comes along! There is, truly, "no force so great as an idea whose time has come," and while those ideas of great magnitude happen very infrequently (for me, at least), I *have* had a few such ideas that catch me up, permeate my being and will not let me rest. Those are the "highs" of the creative life but even in the leaner times the quest for something worthy beckons and one keeps working.

While the process of creativity is somewhat nebulous in nature and hard to define, the *creator* should not, I feel, settle for vague, haphazard or careless treatment of ideas. After a valid thought comes to me and I am attempting to write it into a skeletal text, the "craftsmanship phase" enters the picture and I find myself abiding by *strict* guidelines, which, while partly instinctive, have become my criteria over the years, and the points by which I evaluate not only my work, but also the work of others. To begin with, the Archbishop of Canterbury once delineated four qualities for a good hymn text which I find equally applicable to anthems. These are:

1. A touch of poetry (not necessarily a poem but language that flows)
2. Some teaching incisiveness (meaning a *message* of worth)
3. An "evocative reference" (recalling something familiar from the past)
4. Some personal emotion (involving people's hearts as well as their heads).

The last of these reminds one of Frost's "lump in the throat" and I agree; for when I am in some way emotionally involved in a text and its writing, I am apt to put more and more depth into the song than if it were solely a mental exercise (e.g. "It's All in the Hands of God"). (This is another reason why I don't take commissions: I am

19

most often not in any way *involved* in the particular scenario seeking the commissioned piece.) However, such emotion must be carefully handled lest it become pure sentimentality. This is a very fine line and yet an important one, and one must deal with it sensitively.

In addition to the Archbishop's criteria for a good text, I would add the following:

Good Grammar (No "poetic license" allowed in *this* realm!)

Dignity of Language

Good Taste

Meaning of words today (a "gay" Valentine, e.g.)

Singability (How it "fits in the mouth")

Sound/Beauty of the word

Rhyme and/or Balance (so the ear is satisfied)

Understandability (a "Balm"/bomb in Gilead)

Directness ("Stay" vs. "abide" or "stick around")

Weak vs. Strong words ("smile" vs. "rejoice!")

Correct Syllable Stress (not "je-SÚS," e.g.)

Inclusive rather than exclusive language (God language as well as people)

Until about 1973 (3 or 4 years after I began writing music), I was not conscious of any problem in using traditional language when referring to God, but during the writing of the number about creation for the "Sunday Songbook," my publisher, Don Hinshaw, called my attention to the issue and asked if I would try to re-write the words of the "creation song" in order to avoid "offending" words. This was a difficult thing to do, but I tried and finally succeeded by using the passive voice ("the stars were made"), inferred/indirect action ("the seas arose") etc. Ever since that time I have adopted the criterion of "inclusive language" as one of my guidelines.

20

Explaining how I evaluate the melodies that carry my texts is a harder task because it is mostly instinctive. However, as an Alto for twenty-five years, often called upon to sing very *dull* musical lines, I have made it a point never to write tedious lines for anyone! No matter which part carries the melody, I want my tunes to have interest, direction, "architecture" and shape; and I sing them over and over, refining and amending them until they do. They must also have a reasonable range—which means, in most cases, singable by *me*. The trouble is that I am an Alto, and I tend to write, think, and sing low, so I sometimes have to transpose ideas upward into a more average key for others to sing. Another important factor of the melodies I write is their appropriateness to the thought they carry. For example, I would never write a piece such as the "He Rose From the Tomb Cha-Cha." In my mind the dignity of the glorious Easter occasion would be cheapened and diminished by such an unfortunate combination of ingredients. That is *not* to say that there is only one style of music to which an Easter text may be set, for I do not believe that, and have written several different sorts of Easter pieces myself. But, the fact remains that care must be exercised in writing melodies so that they will support and strengthen the ideas of the texts and not counteract or contradict them.

After I have finished a piece, the next step is evaluating my creative product. This is tricky, but most certainly necessary, even if one ends up throwing out the effort and starting all over again. For me, the first step in the evaluation process is whether or not *I* like it. (If not, forget it, for I certainly cannot expect *others* to think it worthy!) But if I like it and believe in it, so to speak, then I give it a second test which I call the "Test of Time." Rather than sending off a manuscript immediately after the ink is dry, I keep the piece around for a while—say, two weeks—playing it every day several times (and possibly refining it a bit here and there as I play). When I ultimately stop changing it and am happy with the total effort *every time I play and sing it,* I am ready to consider sending it to a publisher.

A third test which I give my pieces is what I call my "Daughter Tape." When I started composing, my daughter was in Jr. High, and whenever she heard me playing (i.e., writing) either a "juicy" chord that seemed "schmaltzy" or a word that seemed at all corny she would say to me: "Oh Mother, NO!" I still hear that voice in my mind/ear when I am composing—especially a piece in which I am deeply "involved"—and I make it a point to avoid the pitfalls which she (and I, too) would find "offensive."

The fourth test for a piece is the publisher's reaction and evaluation, which I welcome and which sometimes raises (minor) points about either tune or text that I have never considered. I ponder such suggestions carefully—though I sometimes reject them. But if I do so, my own reasons for writing a passage the way I did are strengthened by defining and defending them. Presuming that the publisher and I agree that I have written an acceptable piece and that it will be published, the next step—and this is a most *difficult* one—is *letting go.* After it is in print, the song is no longer under my control, but goes out into the world vulnerable to abuse of all sorts, as well as to kind and careful treatment. It hurts the soul a bit to sit in a performance of one's own musical brainchild and hear it "butchered" (for whatever reason), but one simply has to let go, and allow the piece to have a life of its own and the people involved in interpreting and performing it to "do their own thing." I finally adopted a "platonic" attitude towards such experiences, and it has been most helpful. I decided that in my mind, there was an *ideal* vision of how the piece would sound which I would never actually hear in any *real* performance since there is, by definition, a built-in dichotomy between these two poles. Some renditions of my works which I have heard get very close to the ideal; others, not so close, but I feel comforted by the realization that a perfect performance will never happen, and therefore, I can relax a bit. The best thing I can do— as the composer—is to indicate in my manuscript (and later in publication) how the number should be sung, by both metronome number and descriptive adjectives at the beginning of the music ("briskly," "flowingly," etc.). Beyond that, I must simply hope for the best.

In summary, what I am doing—through my composition of both words and music—is more a *ministry* than anything else, and I am grateful that this is the case. It is fulfilling in a total sense, as opposed to simply "filling the time full" with many little, sometimes meaningless activities. It brings together many threads from my past and combines them into a tapestry of life and work which is most satisfying. These include: an interest in poetry; a love of language and how words flow; my beliefs and theology; the "empty nest" time in my life when I am alone; the opportunity to do something beyond myself which can, at best, help other people; and, a sense of purpose and usefulness. I would somehow like to think that the messages of my texts, especially the "inspirational" ones, have the potential for educating, enlightening and enriching people (rather than simply entertaining them), and perhaps, of making them somehow better

23

than they were before they encountered my song. That is a lofty goal, to be sure, but I continue to seek it and to try to write "something worth singing, and something worth singing about."

Natalie Sleeth
Denver, CO.
Summer, 1986

1. Feed My Lambs

This piece really took a long time to "happen"—nearly two years, I think, from the very first related thought to the final song. Leonard Bernstein has a quote about creativity, saying that (for him, and also for me) it's the unexpected and unpredictable/uncontrollable intersection of seemingly unrelated elements that suddenly "catches fire" and produces results. That happened in this case and there were really four factors (over that two-year period) that finally combined to produce the piece. I'll describe them briefly as follows:

First—I saw a (Sunday-School type) poster of a shepherd rescuing a lamb caught in a thicket and I thought it captured a certain warm nurturing, caring feeling and wanted to write about it, but nothing came. Furthermore, I got confused in the theology of the "Lamb" and "Shepherd" image because in the Bible, Christ is sometimes both! So, I abandoned the idea.

Second—One day, many months later, I saw in the Perkins Chapel at SMU a banner with a green (pasture) background and little lambs feeding and at the bottom, the words: "Feed My Lambs" . . . but still no piece happened, even though it recalled my experience (in #1) above.

Third—I struck up a lively correspondence with Katherine K. Davis about this time, and it was so enriching to share "shop talk" that I realized how, through our letters, we were "feeding" each other, and the lambs/feeding/caring took on a *human* aspect. But still no piece.

Fourth—I saw in the ceiling of my own church (where it had always been but I hadn't noticed) the Biblical passage: "Whatsoever ye do unto the least of these, my brethren, ye do unto Me" and suddenly the four stimuli came together and I wrote the essence of the piece!

Because of its pastoral feeling, I scored it for unison choir (a simple setting) and two flutes which suggest a pastoral scene. It took me a long time to "perfect" the counterpoint in the flutes but I finally finished and dedicated it to Katherine K. Davis. She said it was the first piece ever dedicated to her.

Feed My Lambs

Feed my lambs, tend my sheep,
Over all a vigil keep;
In my name, lead them forth,
Gently as a Shepherd.

When they wander, when they stray,
Their protector be.
As ye do unto my flock,
Thus ye do to me . . .

Feed my lambs, tend my sheep,
Over all a vigil keep;
In my name, lead them forth,
Gently as a Shepherd.

Unto all who lose the way
Hope and comfort be;
As ye do unto my flock,
Thus ye do to me . . .

Feed my lambs, tend my sheep,
Over all a vigil keep;
In my name, lead them forth. . . . .
Gently . . . . . . Gently
As a loving Shepherd of the Lord.

2. Spread Joy

This piece is, perhaps, a bit unique because it didn't happen with the words first, but rather, the "feeling" of the music! I remember driving to my job at church with the car radio on playing some peppy, "mod-sounding" commercial (Coca-Cola, perhaps), and also liking the sound of the open fourths and fifths moving around in the musical texture. Then, having that sound in my ears, I went to the room at the church where I normally composed (an hour before my job responsibilities began) and tried to mimic that sort of sound with my own music. I must have captured the essence of it that day, but I had no words, and during the next few weeks, I worked out a text to fit the music, listing lots of verbs and nouns (see below) and finally matching them up into the three "patterns" which the piece contains. (I also remember my daughter and myself getting amused by some of the possible combinations of nouns and verbs that we thought it best *not* to use!)

I don't remember exactly why or how I ended up scoring the song for three parts, but perhaps the nature of the "overlapping melody," which allowed for this treatment, determined the final form of the piece. I also don't clearly recall whether it was my idea or that of Don Hinshaw, my editor at Carl Fischer, to add the trumpet part, but once I thought of that, I had great fun working out that line, trying it out with a local high school trumpeter to find the right mute and discovering just the right sound to add enough "pizzazz" to the piece.

This is a "Pre-Women's Lib Awareness" piece and if I wrote it today, I would avoid the phrase "every fellow *man* you see," but I meant (inclusively) mankind, and my intention was good!

This is one of my favorite pieces because I like the flavor of the music, the message of the words (I'm an optimist and have tried to do the things described in the text) and also the trumpet part when it's played well and with the right mute!

Verbs	Nouns
Bring	Peace
Make	Love
Spread	Joy
Reach	Up
Give	Out
Share	Life
(etc.)	(etc.)

Spread Joy

Spread joy . . . . . Spread joy,
Spread joy to ev'ry *fellow man** you see;
Spread joy . . . . . Spread joy . . . . .
And make the world a better place to be!

Bring love . . . . . Bring love,
Bring love to ev'ry *fellow man** you see;
Bring love . . . . . sweet love,
And make the world a better place to be!

Reach out . . . . . Reach out,
Reach out to ev'ry *fellow man** you see;
Reach out . . . . . Reach out,
And make the world a better place
   for this entire human race,—
Make the world a better place to be,
   For you and me,
   For you and me — to — be!

*Alt.: *"person that"*

3. Baby, What You Goin' to Be?
(two part/four part)

I don't really recall what began this piece, except that it was likely during an Advent Season and I was aware (again) of the Messianic hopes that were age-old (cf. Isaiah) and which expressed the yearning of the people for a Savior. I probably let my imagination wander and recreated that first manger scene with people standing around the newborn baby wondering if it *could* be the special baby for whom they had waited so long.

Actually, there are four "levels" in this text (though one need not attend to them), but they were in *my* mind and I wrote them into the text as well as into the treatment of it. The first "level" is simply that of QUESTIONING: (What You Goin' To Be?). The second level is one of POSSIBILITY: (Do you suppose it *could* be the Messiah

31

we've waited for so long? Probably not but . . . what if?!).
The third level is one of *PROBABILITY,* and comes as the
piece moves on (there *is* something special in this baby—I
can feel it in the air, in the Mother's radiance, in the light
around the babe, etc.). The final "level" is that of *REAL-
IZATION,* which begins after the phrase: "Look now, they
bow unto you" (because why would great Kings do that
for any *ordinary* child?). Musically, this fourth phase is
expressed by the Basses (in the SATB version) coming in
with a very soft (and mystical?) "Hallelujah" and from
that point on, the piece soars confidently to a climax,
dying down in a reverent quiet final section expressing the
awe and wonder of the occasion.

I first wrote this as a solo (with piano), but Don
Hinshaw at Carl Fischer felt there was more to the piece
than merely a solo, and he urged me to try to write a two
part, a three part and a four part version before we decided upon the final form. It took a long time to do this and
each version was an agonizing creative effort but we finally decided on a two-part version *and* a four-part version,
essentially the same, musically, but the four-part is more
intense due to all the counterpoint, commentary in the
subsidiary text, and intensity of sound.

It was thrilling to have the Mormon Tabernacle
Choir put this number on their 1977 Christmas record:
"White Christmas" (Columbia) and to highlight the text
by printing it on the record jacket.

This piece is dedicated to Don Hinshaw because
after all our cooperative work on which version, what
form, etc. (over nearly one and one-half years as I recall)
it was as much his piece as mine. He felt very much the
intensity of the piece and was very moved and pleased to
have it dedicated to him.

Baby, What You Goin' to Be?

Baby, lyin' in a manger,
      slumberin' so sweetly,
      what you goin' to be?
Baby, all the world is watchin',
      all the world awaits to see.

Baby, sleepin' in a stable,
      underneath the heaven,
      what you goin' to say?
Baby, did you bring the Good News,
      did you come to light our way?

Baby, gazin' at the cattle,
      lookin' at the shepherds,
      what you goin' to do?
Baby, will you be the Master,
      will you bring the Kingdom, too?

Oh . . . Baby, hope of all the people,
      what you come to do here,
      what you come to say?
Baby, can you be the Savior,
      come to save the world . . . one . . . day?
Baby, lyin' in a manger,
      will you save the world . . . one . . . day?

4. *God of Great and God of Small*

I don't remember what started me writing this piece but I believe it was the realization of the dichotomy between the all-powerful God and the personal one that cares about even me. So the awareness of the seeming "extremes" of the Divinity (Great/Small ... One/All, etc.) began to form in my mind, resulting in this text. I was glad to "happen on" the phrase "God, whose *love* turns wrong to right" because I obviously couldn't say (and didn't believe): "God of wrong and God of right," which would seem to follow the text pattern I had set up!

I also (providentially?) just "happened on" that key change but it's one of the best ones I've ever written. The hymn-like melody just "came" after I had the words which needed a substantial, traditional, strong-yet-simple, tune to carry them.

The piece is dedicated to my father, though I originally had planned to dedicate it to someone else. However, when my father became terminally ill after Christmas of 1971, I was able to change the dedication (since the piece was not yet published) and to dedicate it to him instead. It was the sort of piece he would have understood. His religion was a very private thing and I thought only a traditional type of piece would be fitting to bear his name (*not* one with syncopation or anything "mod" or innovative). The text was read at his funeral in March, 1972, and I felt glad that he knew the piece would bear his name when it was finally in print.

God of Great and God of Small

God of great and God of small,
God of one and God of all,
God of weak and God of strong,
God to whom all things belong,
Alleluia, Alleluia,
Prais -ed be Thy name!

God of land and sky and sea,
God of life and destiny,
God of never-ending pow'r,
Yet beside me ev'ry hour;
Alleluia, Alleluia,
Prais -ed be Thy name!

God of silence, God of sound,
God in whom the lost are found;
God of day and darkest night,
God whose love turns wrong to right,

God of heav'n and God of earth,
God of death and God of birth,
God of now and days before,
God who reigns forevermore;
Alleluia, Alleluia,
Prais -ed be Thy name. . . .

Prais -ed be Thy name!

5. Have a Good Day

This piece came about because of a poster I had on the wall of my office at Highland Park United Methodist Church, Dallas, when I worked there as a secretary in the Music Department! It was a smiling face (similar to the cover of the anthem) and it said underneath: "Have a nice day." I stared at it day after day, and one day I happened to wonder if there wasn't a way we could all help *make* our days "good days" and not just rely on Fate! Hence, the middle part of the text is a sort of inverse/secular "Golden Rule" which started the whole idea rolling.

I made it a unison piece because I imagined it being used in schools by young choirs, but for interest, I added the flute line. I don't know how often this piece has been sung, but I like the idea of the text and feel good about the message the piece carries.

36

Have a Good Day

Have a good day, a nice day,
A happy day today;
May the sun shine down upon you
And good things come your way.

May a new song, a joyful song
Be in your heart today,
So your burdens all seem lighter
And your troubles melt away.

Now the secret of a happy day is very strange to tell:
Just make somebody else's day a happy day as well;
For when you reach beyond yourself, you'll find that it is
    true:
The love you show will overflow and come right back to
    you.

Then It's a good day, a nice day,
        A special day that day;
        When you make somebody happy,
        Many good things come your way,
        And then a new song, a joyful song
        Is in your heart to stay,
        And the sun will shine upon you
        And you'll find you'll have a hap-py day!

6. Lord, Make Us Worthy

This piece started because of a freshly washed window in my home! I went by the window one day when the sun was shining and it was so clear and clean and "pure" that I started thinking of the verb "washed" and what washing does, even in a liturgical sense of purification. I just went on from there and made a list of verbs, and oriented them to some aspect of Christ's life and ministry, and that eventually became Lord, Make us Worthy. The "Paul" to whom the piece is dedicated, is Paul Spellman, a minister on the staff of Highland Park United Methodist Church at the time, who helped me with the final theological choices of verbs and nouns "matching."

In the text I wanted to do several things: to state (in four words only) a valid and important theological truth, and to combine those so that each "stanza" dealt with a different aspect of Christ, building to a climax the last time through. After each of the "A" sections, I also repeated the prayer-like refrain, "Lord, make us worthy" (of such great gifts as these—ministry, life, etc.). The first four verbs (blessed, touched, graced and fed) deal with Jesus' birth and early life. The second set of verbs (spared, healed, saved, bound, raised) deal more with Jesus' death and resurrection. The middle section is mainly "filler," but tells the story in another way; and the last set of verbs (led, claimed, filled, called) is supposed to be motivational—to give us a task—to follow, to serve, etc. The word "called" particularly has a "so therefore" (what shall we do?) implication—something which I try to write into my texts whenever possible.

38

Lord, Make Us Worthy

Blessed by His coming,
Touched by His birth,
Graced by His glory
Here on the earth,
Fed by His wisdom,
All who believe,
Lord, Make Us Worthy such gifts to receive.

Spared by His mercy,
Healed by His skill,
Saved by His sorrow,
Bound by His will,
Raised by His power,
All who believe,
Lord, Make Us Worthy such gifts to receive.

Sent by the Father, Humbly He came;
Master and Savior, Him we proclaim.
All who have found Him, Now as before,
Offer Him honor and praise . . . evermore,

Led by His Spirit,
Claimed by His love,
Filled with His promise,
Word from above,
Called to His service,
All who believe,
Lord, Make Us Worthy . . .
Each Of Us Worthy . . .
Lord, Make Us Worthy such blessings to receive.

7. Down the Road
(two part/four part)

This piece "happened" one Labor Day rather unexpectedly. I remember being alone at home—an unusual state for a holiday weekend—and sitting at the piano and simply having this idea "come" in fairly full-blown form as I improvised and gave free rein to my thoughts. I think part of the mood of the moment—which resulted in the folklike nature of the music and the "philosophical" content of the words—was the influence of a piece called "Movin' On" by someone named R. Hannisian, which my daughter and I both liked very much and often sang together. Beyond that I cannot pinpoint what "led" to this song, but looking back, it (more than any other of my pieces) expresses my philosophy of life—my acceptance of whatever comes, my faith in the "One who made this road," and my optimism in "knowing the sun is shining though the clouds may hide its beams!"

When I sent the text by itself to Don Hinshaw, he phoned me and said it had had a profound effect upon him, particularly the last phrase of it about hoping it "made a difference that I passed this way," because in his life, that was his hope also. He was anxious to have me add the music, which I soon did, and then he was very pleased with the final piece, which we ultimately decided should be published in both a two-part and four-part version. I still feel good every time I sing or hear this number, and while it is a true statement of my feelings about life (et al.), it doesn't get sentimental or corny. [Which proves something can have "heart" or feeling without crossing the border into an overstatement of feeling.]

It is dedicated to Joyce Eilers, a composer friend, who was going through some hard times in her life at the time and to whom I wanted to give the gift of encouragement by means of the words of this song. She (as well as others) said that she often thinks of phrases from the song and that they help her face what comes. I myself have done this and it is almost as though the whole text had come from "somewhere else" . . .

Down the Road

Goin' to keep on going down the road,
Goin' to hold my head up high.
Goin' to follow where the pathway leads
    till it reaches to the sky,
Goin' to face each joy and sorrow
That I meet along the way,
Goin' to travel out my future day by day.

41

For I know the One who made this road
Is aware of where it goes,
So I follow with my head held high
    ev'ry byway that He chose.
And if I should meet another
At the turning of the bend,
Then the way will go much better with a friend.

Oh I don't know what's ahead of me
At the coming of the dawn,
But I welcome each tomorrow
And I keep a-movin' on;
For my cup is full of promise
And my head is full of dreams,
And I know the sun is shining
Though the clouds may hide its beams. . . .

So I just keep going down the road
And I hold my head up high,
And I follow where the pathway leads
    till it reaches to the sky,
But I hope that where I travel
They will say of me one day:
That it somehow made a difference
    that I passed this way. . . .

That I passed . . . this . . . way.

8. Christmas Is a Feeling

I don't remember what triggered this number but it was during a pre-Christmas season when I was aware that the feeling we refer to as the "Christmas Spirit" is a very special warm, caring, giving feeling, but unfortunately, often limited to one season of the year only. Once I had that beginning, the rest of the words followed naturally, and then the music.

In the accompaniment, to add a seasonal flavor, I "quoted" several Christmas carols! The beginning idea comes from "Angels We Have Heard on High" where the (original) refrain goes "Glooooo-ri-a (etc.)." The rhythm of mine is different, though, so the reference might not be immediately noted. Another "quote" comes in the flute part in m. 24-27, when the melody suggests "There's A Song in the Air." Then that line (flute) goes on to suggest "Away In a Manger" (m. 28-31) and finally goes into a reference to a melody from "The First Noel," though I have (again) changed it a bit. The most exact reference to that carol comes in m. 35-39. Then the piece continues with my original material and in the very end (m. 59-62), the flute refers again to the "First Noel." Hopefully these uses of familiar carols strengthen the "context" for the message of the piece, whether or not the singers and listeners realize where all of the quotes come from.

I added the second part (alto) to make it more interesting for older choirs, though the piece comes off just as well as either a unison choir song or a solo.

Christmas Is a Feeling

Christmas is a feeling
Filling the air,
It's love and joy and laughter
Of people ev'rywhere;
Christmas is a feeling
Bringing good cheer,
It reaches out to touch you
As the holiday draws near.

It's mistletoe and falling snow
And candles burning bright;
It's a baby in a manger
On a cold winter night;

It's glad Noels and chiming bells
And presents by the tree;
It's the spirit of giving
In you and in me,

(For) Christmas is a feeling
Filling the air,
It's love and joy and laughter
Of people ev'rywhere;
But if Christmas is a feeling
Bringing such good cheer,
Then why, O why don't you and I
Try to make it last all year?

Why can't it last . . . all year??

9. The Kingdom
of the Lord

This piece "happened" out of a desire to deal with the concept of the Kingdom, something which is still fairly fuzzy theologically—to others as well as to myself. (Is it here? Is it later? Is it now? Is it in Heaven? Is it both?) I guess I finally concluded that it can be here and now, in part at least, and that you and I can help make it happen by the things we do and the way we live. I just went on from there and wrote it in a folk-like style, and musically, I added a flute to make the texture more interesting. The flute does during the first verse what the second vocal part does in the second verse (when the flute goes on to do something else!).

This piece is dedicated to a friend, Betty Beaty, whose daughter played the flute, and whose friendship was meaningful to me during our later years in Dallas. She was interested in theology and in her church, and I gave this piece to her (in manuscript) the last time I saw her before we moved to West Virginia. Her daughter and I made a tape of it so that she could hear it even if only one voice was singing, along with keyboard and flute. I think she appreciated the gift and the caring behind it.

The Kingdom of the Lord

If you would my disciple be,
Take up your cross and follow me
And together we will bring in the Kingdom of the Lord.

If you would set the world aright,
Then walk with me and seek the light,
And together we will bring in the Kingdom of the Lord.

Where peace shall reign from shore to shore
And love will triumph evermore,

So come with me and find the way,
It lies before us day by day,
And together we will bring in the Kingdom of the Lord.

And together we will bring in . . . .
The Kingdom of the Lord!

10. Were You There on that Christmas Night?

This piece "happened" because two things from my notebook of "bits and pieces" combined unexpectedly one day and caught fire! I was (obviously) searching for an idea and thumbing through one of my notebooks and came to a place where, on the right-hand side of the page, there was an article about spirituals with the Lenten example "Were You There" highlighted in some way so that it caught my eye. On the left-hand page facing this article was something that had to do with Christmas, though

47

seemingly quite unrelated to the article on the right hand page.

Well, the idea of spirituals, and in particular, "Were You There," leaped off the page and allied with the concept of Christmas and I thought ..."Hmm, were you there ... at Christmas time ... on that Christmas night? ... No, of course I *wasn't,* but if I *had* been, what would it have been like?" ... and the piece took immediate shape. I imagined what I would have seen, heard, felt, known, and I had the whole AABA form! The rhythm and nature of the idea and the words "dictated" the melody and I wrote this very fast—meaning the *essence* of text and melodic line. From there on, of course, (each time) there is the refinement phase necessary for every "raw" creative idea—the testing, the polishing of the language, the deciding about other vocal lines and accompaniment, etc. ... but this is challenging and rewarding when the main idea catches hold of you ... and this one did (and still does). I feel excitement every time I hear or sing it and that's an indicator of something. It's a feeling of discovery, a feeling of being entrusted with a rare gift that you must pass on (convey), ... a kind of awakening. Not all ideas are as intense, but this one was, and apparently that feeling is felt by others, too, as I have been told this from time to time.

It is dedicated to "George," my friend, George Shorney, President of Hope Publishing Company.

Were You There on That Christmas Night?

Were you there, were you there
On that Christmas night
When the world was filled
With a holy light?
Were you there to behold
When the Wonder foretold
Came to earth?

Did you see, did you see
How they hailed Him King
With the gifts so rare
That they chose to bring?
Did you see how they bowed
As they hailed Him aloud
At His birth?

Did you hear how the choirs of Angels sang
At the glory of the sight?
Did you hear how the bells of Heaven rang
All through the night?

Did you know, did you know
It was God's own Son,
The salvation of
The world begun?
Did you know it was love
That was sent from above
To the earth?

11. Love Is a Song

This piece came about because we were soon going to make a major move to another (totally strange) part of the country and also into a totally new life-style, and I was wondering if I could (1) really be "me" in the new environment, or whether the "role" that I was to play would prevent that freedom, and (2) whether I would be able to write any music without the stimuli of the preceding years (at Highland Park Church) in Dallas. I "happened on" a quote of Albert Schweitzer which tempered worry No. 2 ("Every man can find on his own doorstep adventures for the soul.") This eased my mind by making me aware that there are stimuli *everywhere* if only I look for them. I had to convince myself (re: worry No. 1) that I could (and *must*) continue to be "me" wherever I am, because unless *I* am content in my heart and soul, I can be of no use to anyone. That idea sort of translated itself into a parallel thought—that I could "sing my song" (live my life/be me) anywhere; and once I thought of that phrase, it grew into the idea "Love Is a Song" that you can "sing" anywhere . . . and this piece was born.

As long as I had ultimately arrived at a non-religious/secular form of the feelings I was expressing, I decided I might as well be totally "secular" in the music, too, and ultimately ended up writing the piece in a ragtime style. I had two volumes of Scott Joplin's music at home—one of piano solos and one of duets—and I remember playing through them both, noting certain typical "breaks," motifs, and patterns, then closing the volumes and attempting to write something original, but in that style. I finally ended up with a long piano "break" in the middle to highlight the keyboard emphasis of Scott Joplin. And I scored the accompaniment for piano duet (two players) since such a ragtime style involves virtually the whole keyboard and quite an able player, if it's a solo performer. Using a duet form meant that two moderately able piano players could perform the piece with a fair amount of ease (and practice) and it seems to have worked! I added string bass and trumpet for heightened interest.

This piece has apparently done very well due to a number of factors (in addition to being a fun sort of number). It received a most euphoric "review" by J.W. Pepper & Son right after publication and that accounted for a big sale in the first year. Also, the scoring of the piece with three melodies made it usable either SSA(SAA) or SAB, enabling all sorts of choirs to make use of it.

I was also interested and pleased that it was used in the Miss Teenage America Pageant in the fall of 1976, and sung by the young men of the First Baptist (Dallas) church choir (under the direction of Mr. Gary Moore) who served as the escorts for the contestants in the pageant. Bob Hope was the "MC" of the Pageant and he even participated in the chorus line while the piece was being sung.

This piece is dedicated "to Ben," who was a trumpeter friend of my son's in the Mustang (SMU) Band, and who helped me finalize the instrumental line by playing it over for me (on several different occasions—each time somewhat amended from the previous time) willingly and without any compensation. His real name is Ben Terrell and I thought it appropriate to "thank him" by dedicating the piece to him.

Love is a Song

Love is a song
That you sing in your heart
With a joyful melody.

You can't go wrong
With a song in your heart;
If you try it, you'll agree!

Sing it high , . . sing it low,
Sing it ev'rywhere you go.
Sing it loud . . . sing it clear,
So that ev'ryone will hear.

For love is a song
And you find before long
It becomes a part of you,

So sing and rejoice,
Put the love in your voice
And sing your whole life through!

12. Joy in the Morning

This piece "happened" one August weekend in Buckhannon, West Virginia and began with the phrase, "Joy In the Morning"—which, it turns out, comes from Psalm 30 though I didn't know that at the time. I may have gotten it out of thin air or from a book I once read by that title; but whatever the origin, the phrase kept recurring to me, and I began to ponder it. As I worked with the idea and with developing the text into a full "statement" (of related ideas) it began to generate more excitement for me, particularly when it "allied itself" to a strong, minor melody with a sequential section in the middle.

I remember working on it all weekend—until very late at night (since I was by myself) and beginning again early in the morning—and enjoying the challenge of working with four parts rather than just the two I often stop with. Perhaps at the back of my mind was the hope that it might prove suitable for an "inauguration anthem" for my husband's inauguration as President of West Virginia Wesleyan College, but that was not uppermost in my mind at the outset. The best (most satisfying) part of writing the whole piece came when I had the idea for the ending with the delayed final major chord. I remember feeling excited at the effect it seemed likely to produce. I also enjoyed the realization that the second time through the material, to avoid a total "repetition" (albeit in another key) I could slow down one part by doubling the note values and achieving a contrast this way—especially by making it (virtually) a capella. So, the nature of the idea itself, plus the wrestling with it, brought about its ultimate form. It was not all conceived from the start by a long shot . . . but that seldom happens anyway.

I wrote out a piano accompaniment and then showed the manuscript to a few people at the college with the idea of its possible use at the Inauguration. But it seemed there would be no keyboard instrument at that occasion and someone suggested "translating" the accompaniment into brass instruments. I did this, with the help of the director of the band at the college, Mr. Dave Milburn, and it was performed at Ron's inauguration in October (22, 1977) with a brass ensemble (two trumpets, two trombones) and the Tour Choir, under the direction of Mr. Jamie Schuppener.

I had listened to a choir rehearsal or two early in the fall (from manuscript) and made a few minor amendments in the score as a result (for better balance of voices and instruments, e.g.) and the piece was finally published in the spring of 1977. I dedicated it to the W.V.W.C. Tour Choir, and put a footnote into the piece, giving credit to Jamie Schuppener as the director of the choir.

This piece has somehow traveled farther than any of mine, except perhaps for Baby, What You Goin' To Be. It has been sung (many times, I understand) by the Mormon Tabernacle Choir over their regular radio broadcasts and by many other choral groups as well. The publisher made available a tape of the accompaniment (no voices), using brass and organ, so that small churches without these resources readily available can still sing the piece.

The cover (front) is very colorful and exemplifies the idea in the text but the back cover is uniquely appropriate to the "place of birth" of the piece, since it is the picture off the college catalog of W.V.W.C., taken in West Virginia not too far from Buckhannon. (The area looks like that!)

54

Joy in the Morning

There'll be joy in the morning on that day,
There'll be joy in the morning on that day,
For the daylight will dawn
When the darkness is gone,
There'll be joy in the morning on that day.

There'll be peace and contentment evermore,
There'll be peace and contentment evermore,
Ev'ry heart, ev'ry voice
Will together rejoice,
There'll be peace and contentment evermore.

And the glory, glory, glory of the Lord
Will shine, . . . will shine (shine upon us)
And the glory, glory, glory of the Lord
Will bring the truth divine.

There'll be love and forgiveness ev'rywhere,
There'll be love and forgiveness ev'rywhere,
And the way of the Lord
Will that day be restored;
There'll be love and forgiveness ev'rywhere.

There'll be love and forgiveness,
There'll be peace and contentment,
There'll be joy, joy, joy, joy, . . . JOY!

13. *Keeping Christmas*
<u>Weekday Songbook</u> (Collection)

After "Sunday Songbook" seemed to meet such a "need" (get a favorable response) in the music world, my publisher, Don Hinshaw, suggested that there was a need for a comparable volume for use in the schools, so "Weekday Songbook" was conceived. The categories were (much) harder to think up than for "Sunday Songbook" (I'm a "theological animal" at heart) because I wanted to say something meaningful and important in the text messages and not simply "entertain." I listed many possible categories, and when I finally got around to beginning work on this volume (in the winter of '77-78 in Buckhannon, West Virginia), I tried one idea after another (some bore fruit and some didn't) and I ultimately ended up with twelve songs in this collection.

One of the numbers, "Keeping Christmas" has a theme or thesis similar to "Christmas Is a Feeling" and it is one of my favorite pieces in the "Weekday Songbook."

Keeping Christmas
(Weekday Songbook)

Let's keep Christmas the whole year through,
Think of all of the good we'd do,
Light the spirit of love anew
    so that all the world might see.

We'd be patient and kind and good,
Understand and be understood,
Treat each other the way we should
    so we'd live in charity.

    Christmas time is a time to care,
    Full of love that you want to share;
    Christmas time is a time to give,
    It's a whole new way to live.

Let's bring Christmas to ev'ry heart,
Love and joy that will ne'er depart,
Each one wanting to have a part,
    what a diff'rence there would be . . .

Let it all begin with you and me!

14. Consider the Lilies

This piece was brought about by two factors, really. The main one was a statement that a young man made about his outlook on life (which was that it didn't matter what sort of job he had as long as he made enough money) and the other was a view out of the back window of our house in Buckhannon, West Virginia of an unmowed field where lots of wild flowers grew and where birds were darting in and out. The phrase "Consider the Lilies" came into my mind, and I worked out the text and later the melody line with an obbligato for either violin or flute.

The piece is dedicated to the young man whose statement "inspired" it ("Jamie"). I thought it might embarrass him if I put his whole name in the dedication because the piece is on the "romantic" side and Jamie was a strong, masculine type who would have avoided anything in his choir work that bordered on the sentimental. I put in the line that the violin (or flute) could play because his fiance played the violin!

I have had several affirming comments about the text and the way it paraphrases the Matthew passage upon which the piece is based. I like to do this in my texts—start with a theological idea, perhaps with a familiar phrase from a Psalm or the Bible somewhere and then "enlarge" upon it, or echo the thoughts in my own words. Examples of this procedure are: "Feed My Lambs," "Joy In the Morning," "The Lord Is My Shepherd" and some others. Choristers Guild even published a sheet as a teaching tool that compares my text and the Matthew passage to see what I omitted.

Consider the Lilies

Consider the lilies and how they grow,
Blossoming there in the field;
'Tis not for their labor they flourish so,
Flowers of beauty to yield.

(Refrain) Through the grace of God above,
Tending all in constant love,
Ev'ry want shall be supplied
For God, the Lord, will provide.

Consider a moment the birds in flight,
Ev'rywhere filling the air.
With never a worry they seek the height,
Nourished in bountiful share.

(Refrain)

Store not up in rich array
Treasures for the coming day;
In the kingdom first believe
And all good things you shall receive.

For more than the lilies that bloom and grow,
More than the birds of the air,
Your Maker forever your need will know
And feed you with Heavenly care.

(Refrain)

God, the Lord,
the loving Lord,
will ev'ry blessing provide.

15. A Little Love

This piece happened in an unusual way and makes me aware of the role of the subconscious mind in the creative process as well as that of the conscious mind.

I keep two notebooks of "bits and pieces" (of stimuli)—poster captions, poems, quotes from one or another source, etc.—and during "lean periods" when no idea is brewing, I look through the books slowly, hoping to have some thought "spring out" at me and start the creative "juices" going. One weekend when I was all alone and had ample time to write a new piece (but no idea for one!) I started trying to get a beginning by thumbing through the notebooks. I found something (I forget what) that seemed promising, closed the books and worked on that idea for most of the day. By nightfall, however, it had not developed so I gave it up, went back to the notebooks and repeated the (thumbing-through) process. I found a second idea which I worked on the next day but it was the same story—by nightfall, nothing—so back to the notebooks. The same thing happened the third day and I was frustrated and discouraged by mid-afternoon, having (in effect) wasted the weekend with nothing "accomplished." Then my husband called from the airport telling me what time he'd be home and between the time of his call (c. 4 PM) and the time he actually got home (c. 6 PM), a totally new idea had "struck," and turned into the essence of this piece—text, melody line, basic musical "setting," et al!

In the course of the next week or so, I had occasion to look back into those two notebooks and found no less than eighteen "stimuli" (scattered throughout the pages) which I wasn't even aware I was noticing . . . but which somehow came together in my subconscious mind and contributed to this piece. I quote some of them below.

This piece is dedicated to "B.B.M. who cares" and that is Betty Bryant Miller, a close friend of mine who exemplifies the things suggested in the text—the reaching out to other people and most of all, the caring.

STIMULI from my NOTEBOOKS that led to this piece:

The love you give away is the only love you keep.

An act of love may tip the balance (poster caption)

Caring must be made concrete; otherwise there is no incarnation, no fleshing out of love.

You don't have to do great things but the little things you are doing in your sphere of influence can be done with great conviction, great wisdom, great beauty and great love.

The door to happiness opens outward.

If we cannot bear another's burden for him, at least we can help to bear it with him.

The impact of love can change lives.

Love is the most powerful force in the world.

Every man is guilty of all the good he didn't do.

Love them now . . . before they're just a guilty memory.

Love is a laugh, love is a look . . .

When, through one person a little more love and goodness, a little more light and truth come into the world, then that life has had meaning.

It isn't the thing you do; it's the thing undone that brings the heartache at the setting sun. . . . The tender word forgotten, the letter you didn't write . . . the stone you might have lifted out of your brother's way . . . the loving touch of the hand; the little acts of kindness, those chances to be helpful. No, it's not the thing you do, but what you leave undone. (Parts of a longer poem.)

If we discovered that we had only five minutes left to say all we wanted to say, every phone booth would be occupied with people calling other people to stammer that they loved them. Why wait until the last five minutes?

I shall pass this way but once. Any good therefore that I can do, or any kindness I can show to a fellow creature, let me do it now. Let me not defer or neglect it. For I shall not pass this way again.

Reach out and touch—a soul that is hungry, a spirit in despair, someone who is lonely, if you care.

The best portion of a person's life is his/her little unremembered acts of kindness and of love.

Our truest gift is something of ourselves.

A Little Love

It only takes a little love to warm an aching heart,
To lift a broken spirit,
To take another's part.
It only takes a little trust, a stranger to befriend,
But oh, it makes a diff'rence in the end.

It only takes a little love to smile a friendly smile,
To touch a grieving shoulder,
To walk a second mile.
It only takes a little time, a kindness to extend,
But oh, it makes a diff'rence in the end.

> He taught us all about it
> So many years ago,
> For love was always with Him
> Wherever He would go.

> He calls us now to follow,
> To take the time to care
> Through all the gentle, loving things
> We share. . . .

(Because) It only takes a little love to calm
         another's fear,
To bear another's burden,
To weep another's tear;
It only takes a little word to cheer a lonely friend,
But oh, it makes a diff'rence in the end. . . .
Oh yes, it makes a world of
         diff'rence . . . in—the—end.

16. Promised Land

This piece is as near to a "commission" as I will probably ever get, though I promised nothing and told them so at the outset.

The "invitation" came from some women seminary students at Garrett Seminary in Evanston, Illinois, who wanted me to write a piece ("like Joy In The Morning," meaning the message, I think) for use at a special conference of Methodist Women in the Clergy in Dallas, Texas, in January, 1979. I told them I wasn't at all sure I could do that, that their (Women's Lib) cause was not necessarily my "number one priority," that I needed "input," etc. . . . but when they gave me some data which included a special service they had written for use that fall at Garrett, it included the imagery of "Promised Land" and "Milk and Honey," with which I, as an optimist, could "tune in."

So . . . I began pondering the project and, after several false starts (and almost abandoning the effort) I finally arrived at the piece, Promised Land.

I wrote it in a spiritual-like idiom to avoid any emotionalism and to give it a vigorous rhythm. In the text, I avoided the pitfalls of "sexist language" by either offering alternatives ("Brothers, Sisters" or "All you Sisters" or "All You Children," etc.) in a couple of places or not even referring to God so that there would be no problem of "masculine pronouns"! The end result seemed to satisfy the women who had requested the piece and, in fact, they were very excited about it, both in prospect and in actuality, and used it as the "keynote" of the Dallas conference where it apparently went over very well.

I wrote this piece to be used first at the conference of Women Clergy in Dallas but not for their exclusive use, writing the kind of text that would be appropriate for almost any sort of setting or performance situation. I really didn't want to be exclusively identified with the Women's "Cause," though I do sympathize with some of their goals, such as full self-development. The publisher cooperated with the timing of publication beautifully so that it was available in print by January 1, 1979!

Promised Land

Brother, Sister, lend an ear,
I'm headin' for the promised land!
Troubles soon will disappear,
I'm headin' for the promised land!
When I reach it there will be
Love and happiness awaitin' for me;
Come along and you will see,
I'm headin' for the promised land!

I'll be singin' freedom's song,
I'm headin' for the promised land!
That's the place where I belong,
I'm headin' for the promised land!
I'll get there one day I know;
Now I've started, I'm a-rarin' to go
Where the milk and honey flow;
I'm headin' for the promised land.

O, listen, don't you hear that trumpet
Sounding forth the call?
O, children, won't you rise and follow,
One . . . and all?

Better days are now in view,
I'm headin' for the promised land!
All my dreams are comin' true,
I'm headin' for the promised land!
Want to leave the past behind,
Face the future with a hopeful mind,
Peace and joy I'll surely find,
I'm headin' for the promised land!

17. The Lord Is My Shepherd

This piece "happened" because of a commission I wouldn't take, but because I hoped to write something appropriate for the situation nonetheless. Mabel Boyter of Atlanta asked me if I would accept a commission for a choral piece for children's voices to be part of a memorial series to honor her husband (Haskell), published by Broadman Press. I told her I never took commissions but that I would certainly try to come up with a piece—within a reasonable time—which would be suitable for inclusion in such a series. I didn't know Haskell Boyter personally, but I knew of his fine work in both church and school music in Atlanta, and I did know Mabel and wanted very much to honor her request. But . . . nothing "came" for a long time—in terms of a text idea (*what* to "say"!).

After working with several (non-scriptural but "religious" in feeling) ideas that just didn't seem to "hit the mark" in terms of being theologically "dead-center" enough, or musically dignified, I almost gave up. But one day I turned to a third, smaller notebook and pondered an "old idea" of using the twenty-third Psalm in a text (I even had a melody for it) which I had previously given up because of the stumbling block of stating it all in language non-offensive to Women's Lib. The natural way to paraphrase the Psalm involved "The Lord is . . . *He*"; and realizing that "in-built" problem in the concept of para-

67

phrasing the Psalm, I gave up (originally). This time—mainly because the subject matter was most totally appropriate for the above-mentioned series—I tackled the project again and finally came up with a text that avoided those offending pronouns. It is not a total "paraphrase" because I have left out a few lines and ideas, as well as adding one or more myself, . . . but it is, indeed, based on Psalm 23.

The "original" music (a minor/modal melody) seemed uniquely appropriate for a setting of this text, and so I re-worked it (with not too much difficulty) and the piece resulted.

I first set the piece with only (solo/unison) voice and keyboard, but then explored other (larger) dimensions of this such as using harp and flute (or keyboard and flute as an alternate) since the textual material as well as the melodic material seemed—in my mind's ear—to be uniquely suited to such a setting. I even met with a harpist (who played over my keyboard accompaniment) before choosing the final setting. I knew that publishing a separate harp accompaniment was pragmatically illogical—too expensive—and not enough situations could have access to a harp. However, those that did could use that instrument and add a great deal to the "richness" of the piece. I finally decided against using a flute and offered only one version of the accompaniment, transferrable from keyboard to harp if desirable (and so marked in the score).

I talked with both Mabel Boyter and Terry Kirkland at Broadman Press (the publisher) and they both seemed pleased with the piece and with the opportunity to include it in the Haskell Boyter Memorial Series for children's voices.

The Lord Is My Shepherd

The Lord is my shepherd,
No want shall I know.
In pastures of green
Where the gentle winds blow,
Beside the still waters,
Wherever I go,
The Lord is my shepherd,
No want shall I know.

The Lord is my shepherd
By night and by day,
Restoring my spirit
In doubt or dismay,
And leading me onward
In righteousness' way,
The Lord is my shepherd
By night and by day.

Yea, though I walk through the valley,
Naught in my heart will I fear;
Safe in the arms of my shepherd,
Comfort and love will be near. . . .

The Lord is my shepherd,
Content will I be,
For goodness and mercy
Shall wait upon me,
Till fin'lly the household
Of heaven I see;
The Lord is my shepherd. . . .
O bless-ed . . . shall . . . I . . . be!

18. Blessed Shall They Be

This piece "happened" because of an invitation from a group of Methodists in Joliet, Illinois, to write a song to be used (in June, 1980) at the retirement of one of the Methodist Bishops in the area. I refused the commission as such (as I always do) but asked them to give me some "input" as to the "thought-content" they desired, plus any other specifics relating to the occasion.

While I used nothing that they sent me, I did eventually come up with the idea of highlighting the theme of *service,* and that made the piece have a purpose to which *I,* also, could relate, as well as making it more generally usable in any choir situation.

I scored it for two vocal parts and keyboard in a Baroque-like style and sent it to AMSI who responded immediately with an acceptance and a contract.

Presuming that the Methodists in Joliet would consider the piece appropriate for the Bishop's retirement, theirs could be the "premiere performance" which would be indicated on the publication by a footnote. I did not plan to dedicate the piece to the Bishop as I did not even know the man—but I planned to mark the occasion in some way with that brief "word" at the bottom of page 1.

Blessed Shall They Be

O bless-ed, bless-ed shall they be
Who serve our God most faithfully;
Who know and do the Lord's command,
And take the truth to ev'ry land.

For they shall be joyful wherever they go;
The fruits of the Spirit within will they know;
Upon them abundance the Lord will bestow,
And through them the glory will shine. . . .

O bless-ed, bless-ed all their days
Are those who join in grateful praise
And serve the Lord who reigns above
To light the world with heav'nly love.

Bless-ed, Bless-ed,
All who serve the Lord above,
Bless-ed, Bless-ed
Who light the world with heav'nly love.

19. The Lord Be With You
20. Only a Baby Came
<u>Laudamus</u> (Collection, Opus 50)

This collection came about because of a suggestion by Don Hinshaw. I had been trying (overly hard, it seems) for some six months or so to write "Opus 50" which I envisioned as having almost cosmic dimensions of some sort—perhaps like a second "Joy In The Morning." I was, however, unable to make it happen and I kept spinning my creative wheels from January to June ('79) with no satisfactory piece resulting. I asked Don to evaluate some of the "wisps" I had tried and "found wanting" and he said—after doing this—that he felt I had much valid material, discarded perhaps too soon, but likely not suitable for my anticipated ("Magnum") Opus 50. He suggested that I review all the fragments of the last six months with an eye towards using those I considered worthy in another form—a collection of shorter numbers—and this eventually became Laudamus.

Not all the pieces included in this volume are "old," however. In the course of re-evaluating the already created musical ideas of the previous six months, other new songs came to mind as well.

I wrote *The Lord Be With You* for my son and his new bride and dedicated the number to them. I had once thought about trying to write a wedding song but that never happened and this took the place of such a song in the sense of wishing them well.

One of the pieces that I especially like and feel good about is *Only a Baby Came*. This came from an old idea that I had gotten off a Christmas card, but somehow it let itself develop in a new context—the collection—in a way that seemed satisfactory. The words are somewhat ironic, reflecting the Messianic hopes for an "earthly King" in contrast to the birth of a simple baby that first Christmas. I improved the words by working on the idea a "second time around" (and modified the accompaniment a bit as well) and it worked.

This collection is not meant to be "another Sunday Songbook." I tried to avoid that by doing several things:
1. I made the content/words more adult in nature than the texts in Sunday Songbook.
2. The accompaniments of Laudamus are more interesting and challenging than those of Sunday Songbook where I always put the vocal melody in the right hand of the piano to make it easier for youngsters to hear and to sing.
3. Also, I had/have no intention of a parallel weekday (secular) volume to "match" Laudamus so that also avoids comparisons with Sunday Songbook and then Weekday Songbook.

The Lord Be With You
(_Laudamus_)

The Lord be with you your whole life through,
In all you say and in all you do,
The Lord be with you and bless you all your days.

The Lord protect you where-e'er you go,
In time of plenty, in time of woe,
And make your life like a joyful song of praise.

Only a Baby Came
(Laudamus)

They waited for a King with crown of gold,
To save the world as was foretold;
A Sov'reign wise, a ruler bold,
But only a baby came.

They waited for a Prince to gain the throne,
A Savior sent by God alone;
A Lord with Kingdom yet unknown,
But only a baby came.

'Twas but a babe who came that night,
The wonder to proclaim;
With brightest star to shed its light
And set the world a-flame!

They waited for a word of truth divine,
A heav'nly Dove, a Sacred sign;
A living branch from Jesse's line,
But only a baby came. . . .

Only a babe to bear the shame,
Only a babe with love His name,
Only a lowly, holy baby came.

21. It's All in the
Hands of God

Although I wrote this piece soon after we first came to Denver, I really had the *idea* back in Evanston in terms of a thesis, and even a skeletal text. I have always liked the Ecclesiastes passage (3:1-10) about "For everything there is a season" and that had been in the back of my mind as something I hoped to write a piece about—"someday." Then it "allied" itself to an experience I had involving the death of a good friend, Jack Green (former football coach of VU when we were there), because I realized that during his long (fourteen months) struggle with the effects of a malignant brain tumor, he had accepted his "fate," and met what he had to go through with faith and courage. After his death, his wife (whose support echoed that same sort of faithful acceptance) wrote us a letter in which she quoted that very phrase from Ecclesiastes: "For everything there is a season." Both of these factors combined to enable me to begin concretely to work on the piece during our early weeks in Denver.

While the text is "based on" the Ecclesiastes passage, it is not strictly "taken from" that portion of Scripture. There are many thoughts in the original that I did not want to "highlight" or include in my words ("a time to hate," e.g.) so I only took a few of the phrases that I did like and then added some of my own and wove them together with enough "references" to the original to suggest the Biblical source.

I experimented with key, with modulation from one key to another, and finally—after the publisher seemed to prefer the key of FM to EbM—left it there. I worked a long time to arrive at what I considered the "proper ending," having written out both a longer version and a shorter version than the published piece has. As to the format of the piece, I avoided the "trap" of strict repetition of an AABA form by "truncating" the accompaniment between Voice II's first two statements, and also by not stating the entire "Theme II" by itself, but letting Voice I re-enter in the middle section when it occurs the second time through. This saved the piece from being tedious, I think, and made a nice contrast.

While not exactly a "dedication," I did put under the title: "In Memoriam—JFG," as a tribute to Jack. I chose the title and thesis of the piece as representing (1) the *ideas* of the Scripture (though not the exact words) and also (2) my own philosophy/theology that our life (in the larger sense) and what happens to us is not due either to "our doing" or just left to fate, but somehow reflects the Maker's Plan for us. We do not always understand why things happen; nor can we imagine the timing of the events in the future, or explain the timing of things past. We can only live, day to day, confident that there *is* a plan for each of us, and that our destiny is ". . . in the hands of God" (meaning, of course, under the control of God).

77

It's All in the Hands of God

There's a time for living and a time to die,
A time for laughing and a time to cry,
A time for wondering and knowing why,
But it's all in the hands of God.

There's a time for harvest and a time to sow,
A time for happiness, a time for woe,
A time for lingering, a time to go,
But it's all in the hands of God.

> For ev'rything there's a season,
> Since first the world began;
> For all that is there's a reason,
> It's part of the Maker's plan.

There's a time for singing and a time to pray,
A time to gather and to cast away,
A time for ev'rything that comes our way
But it's all in the hands of God.

It's all in the hands of the Lord, our God.

22. Bought With a Price

I can't pinpoint exactly what brought forth this piece, but it grows out of my belief that, because I am a Christian, the crucifixion (et. al.) should make a difference to me. The phrase from St. Paul about being "bought with a price" intrigued me, and I simply added to that, one line at a time, until I had a text that made sense.

The middle part, which stems from a Micah passage, is something I had been trying to find a way to use for a long time but could not, mainly because the original Micah quote has the sort of "syntax" that uses (or implies) exclusive language, which I try to avoid. But I had thought of a four-line paraphrase some time before the "Bought with a price" idea occurred to me and when I began to write this piece, the Micah lines seemed a logical middle part to contrast with the "bought" idea; so I used it.

While "Saved by the blood of the Lamb" is, in a way the most climactic phrase of the text, I did not want to use that as the title. If I had done so, it would have suggested that the piece was of a wholly different sort than it is, and I wanted to avoid the (second born) connotations implicit in those words. But it was part and parcel of the concept of being "bought with a price" and so I wanted to include this in a convincing and crucial way.

I spent a long time "perfecting" the text because I was dealing with important theological concepts and didn't want to treat them lightly. Also, in the second voice, I wanted to get across the same ideas but with fewer words, so I had to work to find some way to say it all. I am basically pleased with the final result.

What I enjoyed most about the whole piece (besides highlighting the thesis) was the Bach-like accompaniment motive that appears at the beginning, at the "break" (and key change) and at the end. It was great fun working with that and figuring out how to use it!

I felt this piece was best left as two-part, since the message of the words is important, and too much contrapuntal activity might detract from that element. This way the piece can be used by trebles only (in two parts), or by Men contrasting with Women, which gives a greater variety of possibilities than SATB would have.

Bought With a Price

You were blessed by the Word,
Born of the Spirit
Called by the Pow'r Divine.

You were led by the light,
Washed with the water,
Marked by a sacred sign.

You are part of the Chosen People,
You are Children of Abraham,

You were bought with a price,
Spared by a sorrow,
Saved by the blood of the Lamb.

So what, then, does God require of you?
Nothing in truth you cannot do:
This, this alone your whole life thru
But to walk in the way of the Lord!

You were claimed by a cross,
Graced by a glory,
Loved by the Lord on high.

You were fed by the faith,
Filled from the fountain,
Destined to testify.

You are part of the Chosen People,
You are Children of Abraham,

You were bought with a price,
Spared by a sorrow,
Saved by the blood of the Lamb!

Bought with the price
Of a sacrifice and
Saved by the *blood* of the *Lamb!*

23. O Come, O Come, Immanuel

Since I had never written a "Christmas piece" for Choristers Guild, when their "turn" came around again, I set out to try to do just that. I "spun my creative wheels" for at least two weeks over a series of short (4-8 m.) phrases (fragments), several of which seemed enticing at first but refused to develop. One was even entitled "O Come" (etc.), and proved to be a canon (four times) but it didn't seem to want to go anywhere *else* after it "canoned" so I dropped that. But still I kept on. Later, while going over these fragments, particularly the "O Come" text-thought, I slowed it down and led into the idea differently, and suddenly it seemed to move forward and to have a great deal more depth than the above-mentioned "ditties," so I persevered and this piece is the result.

As it was developing, it took on a much larger and more mature framework than merely a "Children's Christmas piece" (Angels/Shepherds/Wisemen—and an Oom-Cha beat!) and I began to think of Doreen Rao's wonderful Glen Ellyn Children's Chorus with its "English Boy Choir sound," a setting which seemed appropriate for the piece. I had long wanted to dedicate a piece to Doreen and her chorus, but nothing before this number seemed right. This, however, I could virtually *hear* performed by that group, so I did decide that it should bear her name.

This piece "came" very quickly, once I got started, and I might almost say that it seemed to write itself, by which I mean that I agonized and rewrote very *little,* almost "hearing" each chord as the melody moved along. The harmonies are richer than most of my pieces and I am glad for that fact. The intensity of the feeling of the text idea—"O, Come . . . O *Come,*" almost a pleading— helped these colorful accompanimental sounds evolve.

While the melody of the descant could (conceivably) start at the beginning (because it also "matches" the first and second verses) I decided to leave the piece Unison (against the rich chords) until the last half of the middle section, then bring in part two against the first part, and finally, have it "soar" as a descant with the final melodic statement. I feel this works out well, and adds excitement and depth to the end of the piece. The "Coda" settles it all down, sensitively, into a statement of the Messiah bringing love to earth, a fitting place to end, it seemed. The "Division" of the Descant gives a nice three-part chord on the final note, and puts it all to rest.

O Come, O Come, Immanuel

O come, O come, Immanuel,
Come now to earth and with Thy* people dwell;
The world awaits from heav'n a holy sign,
O come and show to us the light divine.

O come, O come, Immanuel,
As age to age the prophets did foretell;
Redeemer, come, to save us one and all,
Be born again in Bethl'hem's manger stall.

For Thy* coming we prepare,
Wisdom from on high;
Gracious Spirit, Lord most fair,
Now to us draw nigh;

O come, O come, Immanuel,
And free Thy* children: Israel;
Be now our hope, our comfort from above,
And bless us all with everlasting love.

*(Alt.: "your")

© 1982 by Choristers Guild
Used by permission.

24. Psalm

This piece came about somewhat unexpectedly but—when it did—it was further "proof" that it was based on an idea *"whose time had come"* and that it could not have "happened" before that time!

In June of 1982 we moved into a lovely tenth floor apartment in Denver with a "view" of the mountains and one of our friends commented to me that sometime I should try to write a piece based on the idea "I will lift up mine eyes" from the Psalms (121, I think it is). After we got "settled" and I had finished a few other projects, I *did* turn my attention to trying to do just that but it did not work. My text efforts (and consequent melodic ideas) took a syncopated turn and I knew *that* did not "fit the mood" of the (pastoral?) psalm, so I put it all aside as a "learning experience" and went on to something else.

In December of '82, however, I heard that the Mormon Tabernacle Choir was going to sing a piece of mine (Christmas Festival) both "in concert" and on their A.M. radio broadcast (of 12/19/82) and my husband arranged—as my surprise Christmas gift!—for us to go out to Salt Lake City to hear the choir render the number "in person." After working out details (and pondering such an idea for a few days to get used to it!) I agreed. We did make the trip, and it was a wonderful experience all around. While we were there (especially while flying into Salt Lake City), I had a feeling of the nearness of the mountains, as Salt Lake City is more or less in a "bowl" with mountains all around. In addition, the whole weekend with the Mormons was certainly a *"mountain-top"* experience; furthermore, the Associate Director, Donald Ripplinger (my friend and contact) even said to me as we were leaving: "You ought to write about the mountains sometime. . . ." So, all those seemingly diverse "iron filings" suddenly came together, and when I got home to Denver, I tried again. This time it worked.

I used the Psalm phrase as a "springboard" (only) and still avoiding exclusive language, worked the idea into an AABA form as follows:

A   I will lift up mine eyes (to the hills)
A   I will lift up my heart (to the Lord)
B   The Lord is my keeper . . .
A   I will lift up my voice (singing praise)

I also "elongated" the lines in a manner that avoided any "syncopation" and created a gentle, quiet feeling appropriate to the Psalm which I liked.

I sent it to Bob Wetzler at AMSI and he wrote back—by return mail—that he liked the piece very much and indeed wanted to publish it! The only thing we "disagreed" on was the title. I wanted to call it, simply, "Psalm" because it was not any particular (numbered) Psalm, and any adjective that I tried to add sounded "hokey." (Quiet Psalm, Serene Psalm, Pastoral Psalm, etc.). So—I wrote back to Bob and "explained" why I had settled on just "Psalm" and he ultimately agreed! I also dedicated it to Donald Ripplinger, but I did so with initials only, so that it would not all be a "public thing" and so that I would also avoid any possible "embarrassment" to him. It reads simply, "To D.H.R.—in appreciation" (or words to that effect). I feel good about the piece and the way it happened and I also "wrote a lot of myself" into this number.

Psalm

I will lift up mine eyes,
Lift mine eyes to the hills,
To the mountains whence cometh my help,
To the mountains and hills
Far away.

I will lift up my heart,
Lift my heart to the Lord,
To the Lord who made Heaven and earth,
I will lift up my heart
Day by day.

    For the Lord is my Keeper,
    Nevermore shall I fear;
    Though the darkness surround me,
    I will be of good cheer;

I will lift up my voice,
Singing praises alway,
Joyful praises to God evermore,
For the Lord is my strength
And my stay.

    I will lift up mine eyes. . . .
    Lift my heart and my voice,
    To sing praise and rejoice
    Alway.

Cantate

(A Collection of Eight Songs for Three Parts)

I don't remember exactly when Don Hinshaw first mentioned to me his hopes that I would write another collection, more-or-less patterned after "Laudamus" but for three parts instead of two, but that was the impetus behind my trying to write such an opus in the fall of 1983. I asked him to tell me which three parts (SSA/SAB/etc.) he had in mind, but he said he thought I should deal with that as the pieces developed (which I did) and some turned out best sung one way and some, another. That potentially makes the collection (pieces) usable for more and varied groups and, rather than being a drawback, it seems an asset.

When writing a collection such as this I usually start with the key seasons of the church year and hope to write a number for each of those. The other numbers could, conceivably, be general and yet, I didn't want to "repeat" exact ideas from any other opus I had written, and also wanted to try to include a few pieces on subjects which I had never written about before. So . . . I began, and eight items are included in this book. Once I got started on the project, the ideas developed fast and I had finished all eight by Thanksgiving (about three months' work). Fortunately the eight proved to be enough material for the collection because had they not, I was apprehensive that my creative "surge" would not return after interrupting it for Thanksgiving, two trips, Christmas, etc. But the eight seemed to constitute a complete volume, and I was grateful for that.

25. Comfort Ye (Advent)

This was a new idea for this collection and the text thought is from the Isaiah passage which I have always liked. The main problem I had in writing it was that my original idea was *two* parts only (the melody and its "canon") and I had a hard time dreaming up a decent third part to go with the others; first I had it in the second Alto range but Don Hinshaw "edited" it into a baritone range instead, which made more sense.

26. Behold the Shepherd (Lent)

I have always had trouble writing about Lent . . . probably for several reasons: first, being an optimist, it is hard for me to state (well) a minor/tragic/sorrowful message. Second, there are many diverse moods of the Lenten Season: from the joyous processional of expectation on Palm Sunday, to the quiet, meditative Last Supper of Maundy Thursday, to the sorrow of the cross on Good Friday, and finally, to the joy and celebration of Easter Sunday. (Not all of those are technically a part of Lent but my point is clear; it is difficult to write a piece appropriate for and usable during only "ten minutes each year"!) But, I needed to have a piece that dealt with that theme, so I read the concordance and looked up the various passages on "shepherd"—as well as looking through my "notebook of bits and pieces—and I ultimately found a "thesis" that "caught fire" ("content to suffer for his sheep") and wrote this piece. In a way, it is an allegory—which I realized only after I wrote it! I think I put more of

89

"myself" into this number than into any other in the book and the "depth of feeling," especially in the *MISERERE* sections, still affects me when I sing it. I have never heard this piece performed and I somehow hope that I can do so at some point in the future.

27. Break the Bread (Communion)

This is, in a way, an "old idea" (too) which I had had when aiming in quite another direction, but jettisoned before I really gave it a chance to develop fully. However, the melody kept "haunting" me and a phrase or two of the words as well, so I looked at it again—many months later—and considered it for this collection. I remember working out the words (only) in Aspen in July of 1983 (when my husband and I spent a week there) and once I had those "set," the rest was easy! (My usual pattern!) The melody was instinctively in my mind already (the old tune) and I had only to add two other parts (to complement it) to complete the piece. I ended up feeling very satisfied with the whole number, for the "essence" of a (possibly mystical) communion experience is hard to "write down."

28. For the Joy of Music
(General/praise/thanks)

The melody of this piece was also an "old" wisp that never got off the ground but when I looked at it anew and combined it with a new thought (about which I had also tried to write before but had not succeeded), it seemed to "work"! The idea of being thankful for music and all its outlets certainly "rings true" for me, and that "involvement" started the "ball rolling." The strong three/four rhythm is also a nice contrast to a number of four/four pieces in the collection and propels the message forward with something of an "impact."

29. The Fruits of The Spirit
(Pentecost/general)

I have never written about the "Spirit" before (though I have tried) and it is, at best, a "fuzzy" concept to verbalize, much less to "condense" into a piece and to sing! But I tried—no less than three times—to find a way to deal with it, and the third time, it worked! (The first two efforts dealt with the idea by asking "What is the Holy Spirit?" and then "What does it do?" and those are impossible questions to answer so I never got past "first base"!) I finally returned to the Concordance, and then to the Bible and when I read again about the "fruits of the Spirit" I felt I had finally found a way to "say it"! From that moment on, it developed fast and with real vigor and I felt good about it as a part of the collection. It was sung (from manuscript) at a Chapel Service at Iliff Seminary (in Denver) on May 10 of 1984 when my husband and I, together, led worship which consisted of him reading Scripture and I, reading (or having sung) some of my texts based on those Biblical passages. The piece is dedicated to "Ralph" and that is another story! When in Chicago in the 1980's I had a friend with the Lyon & Healy Music store in the "loop" with whom I had lunch periodically. She once told me about a friend of hers who was quite religious, who called the Holy Spirit "Ralph." While that sounds at first sacrilegious, I think that it's rather a delightful way of indicating the closeness of the Spirit as a comfortable and familiar part of one's life and being . . . so I began, too, to think of the Spirit in that way and to refer to him as "Ralph." While trying to write this piece about the Spirit, then, and seemingly getting nowhere (fast), and then having it suddenly take hold and make sense, I decided that "Ralph" was surely present and that I must, indeed, dedicate the song to him. Only my friend from L&H and a few others know about this but I feel the presence of "Ralph" was crucial to the birth of this number.

25. Comfort Ye
(Cantate)

Comfort ye, Comfort ye,
Listen and hear:
Soon the Anointed of God will appear;
The time is at hand
And the hour is near;
Comfort ye, Comfort ye,
Be of good cheer!

    Behold, a Virgin shall conceive,
    Awake! Arise! Rejoice! Believe! (and)

Comfort ye, Comfort ye,
Listen and hear:
Soon the Anointed of God will appear.

    Ev'ry valley shall be exalted,
    Ev'ry mountain and hill made low;
    Yea, the wilderness, too, shall blossom,
    All the land with joy o'erflow. . . . so . . .

(repeat first section—and then end:)

Comfort ye. . . .
Comfort ye. . . .
God . . . is . . . near!

26. Behold the Shepherd
(Cantate)

Behold the shepherd on the hill;
He tends the flock while all is still,
He scans the height and probes the deep,
Content to suffer for his sheep.

Behold what burdens he must bear,
The wayward lambs within his care;
He watches well while others sleep,
Content to suffer for his sheep.
    Miserere, miserere, miserere nobis
    Miserere, Lord, have mercy,
        Grant to him Thy peace.

Behold his love for one and all,
His sacrifice for great and small,
A lonely vigil he must keep,
Content to suffer for his sheep.

All we like sheep have gone astray,
But Christ would shepherd us alway,
And for our sins in sorrow weep,
Content to suffer for his sheep.
    Miserere, miserere, miserere nobis,
    Miserere, Lord have mercy,
        Grant to us Thy peace.

27. Break the Bread
(Cantate)

Break the bread, drink the wine,
Holy feast, sacred sign;
Lamb of God, love divine
Shed for me.

Sorrow's cross now recall,
Christ the Lord died for all;
Faithful folk, great and small,
Thankful be.

Bend the knee, sin confess,
Humble hearts now express,
Mercy-filled, God will bless
Graciously.

Rise and go, born anew,
Purified through and through,
Evermore good pursue
Joyfully.

28. For the Joy of Music
(Cantate)

For the joy of music,
For a voice to sing,
For a song to praise Thee,
Thanks, O Lord, we bring.

For the mighty trumpet,
For the tuneful string,
For the pipe and cymbal,
Thanks, O Lord, we bring.

Some may offer treasure,
Build a temple high,
But with music's measure,
We will magnify!

For the sound of singing,
Bells that loudly ring,
Instruments in chorus
Thanks, O Lord, we bring.

For the joy of music thanks we bring!!

29. The Fruits of the Spirit
(<u>Cantate</u>)

"I will pour out my Spirit,"
Saith the Lord, "from on high.
And the young shall see visions,
And the old, prophesy!

All your sons and your daughters
Shall grow strong and increase,
For the fruits of the Spirit
Shall be love, joy and peace."

"I will pour out my Spirit,"
Saith the Lord, "day by day,
And all those who receive it
Shall in truth find the way!

From their woe and their sorrow
They shall soon know release,
For the fruits of the Spirit
Shall be love, joy and peace."

"I will pour out my Spirit,"
Saith the Lord, "evermore.
And the faith of the people
Once again I'll restore.

They shall hope for the Kingdom
Where delights never cease,
For the fruits of the Spirit
Shall be love, joy and peace."

"Yes, the fruits of the Spirit
shall be love and joy and peace!"

30. Happy Are They

I first thought of the title/thesis of this piece while on a cruise, relaxing, and I think its original form comes from the Bible and says something like "Happy is the *man* who trusts" . . . etc. However, I did not want to use *that* form so I changed it and broadened it to "they."

When I pondered (both on the cruise and after we returned home) how to go on with the above phrase, I kept getting nowhere, and painted myself into a corner, poetically, and couldn't get out . . . so I abandoned the idea and went on to work on something entirely different. But—that alternate idea didn't work either—and I kept finding myself waking up in the morning (Winter, '85) singing/saying "Happy are they who trust in the Lord" and one day I said to myself: "OK. Now just work on that

and perhaps your 'craftsmanship' can make it develop."
Fortunately I did find a way and worked out a complete
text in one day, which started the piece on its way.

At the same time I noticed the inspiring "witness" of
a man in Denver—whom I knew only slightly but respect-
ed and admired greatly—who was facing imminent death
from terminal cancer but who showed an attitude of faith
and trust as well as acceptance of what was ahead for
him. Since he was a public figure in Denver, there were
several articles about him in the papers as well as a TV
special ("Profile in Courage"). I found all of this most
moving, so I felt I wanted to dedicate the piece to him
when I finished. This was done, but only with initials; the
man's name is Dale Tooley, and the dedication reads
simply "For R.D.T."

Remembering all that this man was going through
(as I was writing the piece) and, perhaps, hoping to
state—in a way other than just "Sleeth"—the idea of
trusting in God, I chose to make the middle section of my
piece a complete "quote" of the early American hymn:
"God Is My Strong Salvation." The tune is strong and
familiar and the original words said exactly what I wanted
to say in the piece. So that is what I did, and the result was
a nice, usable anthem with an "anchor" in the past as well
as in the present.

The man to whom I dedicated the piece attended the
St. Thomas Episcopal Church in Denver and I had been
there often and knew the choir director, Bob Johnson,
very well indeed. So, after I had written the anthem and
heard from the publisher that he liked it, I told Bob J.
about it and he planned to teach it to the choir immediately and to perform it on Palm Sunday, '85, while Dale
Tooley was hopefully still alive. Only the choir, the choir

director (Bob J.), the head pastor of the church, Dale Tooley and I knew that it was dedicated to him and I wanted it to be this way so there would be no big "fanfare" about the performance which might cause Dale any embarrassment, or strain. But he did know about it all (as I wrote him) and said he was very pleased that I wanted to do this.

The piece was premiered Palm Sunday, March 31, 1985 and Dale Tooley died the next day. I had a phone call from his daughter the day after that and she said she had sung the piece to her Dad the night before he died, and he liked it so much.

Dale's funeral was on Wednesday of Holy Week, and I attended. As one of the "prelude" numbers before the service began, the organist (Bob Johnson, again) played (at a slightly less than sprightly tempo) "Happy Are They," which—with the hymn middle—seemed to fit quite well.

The next day I received one of the most beautiful letters I have ever received from his daughter, Kyla, telling me how much my "outreach" (in several forms) had meant to Dale, and it truly warmed my heart.

Perhaps all of this "story" was for me a "preparation" of things "closer to home" which soon followed.

Happy Are They

Happy are they who trust in the Lord
And cheerfully God obey;
Led from above
By Heavenly love,
Their feet will not go astray.

Happy are they who trust in the Lord
And lift up their voice in praise;
Joy will they know
Wherever they go,
And thankfulness all their days.

In time of pain or sorrow
They know the Lord will lead,
And ev'ry new tomorrow,
Will for their needs provide . . .

Happy are they who trust in the Lord
And gratefully God adore;
All who believe
Will blessings receive,
Both now and forevermore.

*God is my strong salvation,
What foe have I to fear?
In darkness and temptation,
My light, my help is near.
Though hosts encamp around me,
Firm in the fight I stand.
What terror can confound me
With God at my right hand?

Hymn: WEDLOCK; words by James Montgomery

31. All Good Gifts

This piece came about because of an invitation to my husband and me to do a "double-header" weekend at Christ United Methodist Church in Pittsburgh, PA, in mid-October of 1984 (with Ron preaching and me doing something musical). My friend from former Dallas days, John Erickson, was the organist at C.U.M.C. and was involved in planning the weekend as part of the church's thirty-fifth anniversary celebration. John asked me (way ahead of time) if it might be possible for me to write a special new piece that the choirs could premiere while we were in Pittsburgh and that was the motivation for my creative effort which ultimately turned out to be "All Good Gifts."

Although it may seem surprising, it took me six months and five tries (duds) before this piece actually came about. This was partly because I wasn't immediately able to decide what I wanted to say in the words (message) and that, for me, is the first step to any new anthem. I contemplated various possible themes and worked on each for a while, trying to make it develop, but ultimately discarded them, one by one, as not being quite right—both as a piece and for Christ UMC's anniversary. (However, I did not want to write anything that was only appropriate for that situation alone but a piece which could have general use as well as being uniquely appropriate in

Pennsylvania.)

One morning—after I had been "trying" for a long time—I woke up with the refrain running through my head:

> All good gifts cometh from the Lord,
> Cometh from the Lord in great array;
> All good gifts cometh from the Lord,
> Cometh from the Lord God day by day.

And I thought to myself: "That's it! That's what I want to say in the words—although a lot more as well" and so I went to work and wrote some words and music that preceded that refrain as well as followed it and I had the beginnings of a piece! In the middle I decided to use "Old 100th" (Doxology melody) but with my words, and at the end, the Shaker tune, "Simple Gifts" because both of those evoked feelings of "thanks" and "gifts" and furthered the theme I was writing about.

The piece was premiered during our October "double-header" weekend in 1984, though it was sung from manuscript as the publisher couldn't have it in printed form that quickly (it was published in April '85). However, the publisher allowed the church to photocopy the engraved proofs which made the piece much more legible for the choir to read than my manuscript would have been. "All Good Gifts" was sung both in the morning service and in an afternoon concert and went very well both times. It should prove to be usable on many occasions by other churches as well.

I did ask that a note be put on the bottom of the first page of the anthem saying "First sung at Christ United Methodist Church, Pittsburgh, PA, on Sunday, October 15, 1984"—or words to that effect.

All Good Gifts

On this day of days
Join in grateful praise
That will sound from shore to shore,
And for blessings all,
Whether great or small
Offer thanks forevermore!

All good gifts cometh from the Lord,
Cometh from the Lord in great array.
All good gifts cometh from the Lord.
Cometh from the Lord God day by day!

Special gifts have we
In variety
By the Spirit's grace inspir'd.
But to all so blest
Shall be put the test
For of them is much requir'd!

All good gifts cometh from the Lord,
Cometh from the Lord in great array.
All good gifts cometh from the Lord,
Cometh from the Lord God day by day!

Let ev'ry heart anew prepare
Thru all the world these gifts to share,
In praise to God who reigns on high,
To bring the Heav'nly Kingdom nigh.

Let those who will, glad anthems sing,
Or words of healing comfort bring,
Let others preach or prophesy,
The Lord our God to magnify. . . .

Let your light so shine,
Use your gifts divine
That wherever you may go,
You reflect the love
Of the Lord above
In abundance here below.

All good gifts cometh from the Lord,
Cometh from the Lord in great array.
All good gifts cometh from the Lord,
Cometh from the Lord God day by day.

Many gifts we are given from the time of our birth
By the Lord our God who ruleth o'er the earth;
Great joy ever after shall be our true reward
If we use our talents to serve the Lord!

32. How Will They Know?

This piece came about in the late spring and early summer of 1984—partly in response to a request from the Mormon Tabernacle Choir people and partly in answer to a wish from Sonos Music Resources for a "dose of Sleeth," perhaps to give a shot in the arm to this "in-house" (Mormon) publishing company. They wanted me to write them some music and they named as their preferred "slots" such occasions as Mother's Day, Patriotic songs and Thanksgiving—all hard assignments to fill (for me!).

When I finished another project and was ready to begin pondering possibilities for Sonos, I became aware, through watching our son, Tom, "parenting" his little boy, Michael, of the responsibility and influence we had had as parents on Tom and thus on Michael as well. While Tom and his wife are doing a good job of parenting, the *fact* that they are raising children brought to my mind both the good and not-so-good things that my husband and I might have done (or not done) when *we* were parenting, and I thought of the "thesis" of the piece:

"How will they know *unless we teach them so?*"

Once I had that idea, the rest wasn't too hard to develop because I merely tried to highlight what the best things were that we could try to impart to our children—

though this could also be as a good teacher, grandparent or whatever capacity enables us to influence "the ones for whom we care" as the lyric says. I also offered an alternate text at that spot ("these babes") because I feel the piece is usable on such occasions as Mother's Day, Father's Day, Baptisms and even for "commissioning" church school teachers, for example. Hence, the alternate is given.

Musically, there was a lot of work involved in getting this number into its final form because Jerold Ottley, Director of the Mormon Tabernacle Choir apparently liked both the text and the melody but said my "arrangement" was not really "workable" with a choir of 375 voices. So (and all this was "translated" to me by the non-musician publisher!) I was asked to try to re-write the piece with only the vaguest of "clues" as to *how*; but I did try to clarify the counterpoint and perhaps to make it more "lush" (four-part rather than three) at certain points as well. Fortunately Jerold Ottley liked my revised version and with a minimum of suggestions (which came from the Mormon Tabernacle Choir's arranger and composer, Bob Manookin), mainly about making the accompaniment more "organistic," the piece was accepted for publication *and* put in the "Mormon Tabernacle Choir Performance Library"—which is an added "bonus."

I dedicated the number to our grandson, Michael, because it was through watching him being guided by our son Tom and his wife that I thought up the idea of the piece in the first place. I received a tape of the Mormon Tabernacle Choir singing this number and gave it to Michael for his records. It was premiered on May 12, 1985—Mother's Day—and the performance was dedicated to the memory of my late husband, Ron.

How Will They Know?

How will they know,
  *these babes** for whom we care,
That God is love,
  and with us ev'rywhere,
That life is good,
  with blessings all can share?
How will they know unless we teach them so?

How will they learn,
  that tho' they go astray,
God will forgive
  and help them find the way?
How will they feel
  the Spirit day by day?
How will they know unless we teach them so?

  How will they grow in wisdom and delight?
  How will they choose to follow what is right?
  How can they trust their future will be bright?
  How will they know . . . unless we show them?

How will they live
    when they at last are grown?
What will they give
    to children of their own?
Will they reflect
    the values we have shown?
How will they know as on they go?
How will they know unless we strive to teach them so?

*Alt: *"The ones"*

33. Ev'ry Child

This piece occurred to me because two friends of mine on the pastoral staff of Wellshire Presbyterian Church (who share the Youth Minister's job) named their new-born baby daughter after me—Natalie Jeanne Meyer! Somehow that was *very* special to me and I decided I <u>had</u> to try to write some kind of a piece relating the birth of Jesus to the birth of any/every baby. That thesis is potentially dangerous, however, because it can get into presumptions, theologically, that verge on the extreme (and on the untrue). However, being aware of that pitfall, I attempted to work out a text which only suggested similarities and therefore was acceptable theologically. I checked it with my friend, Schubert Ogden (theologian at SMU/Perkins) and he found no problem with the words, so I went ahead with the project.

After I had finished writing the first part (once through the whole text) I decided that those were not words that *children* would sing so I "programmed" that section (as well as its repeat later on) for "Youth or Adult Choir," though still in unison. Then I inserted in the middle a section to be sung by a Children's Choir, which uses the familiar Christmas carol, O Come, Little Children, though I adapted the words so that their content "fit" my thesis. This would allow "combined choirs" to render the piece at a Christmas program and it seemed, therefore, especially usable to the publisher.

The "capstone" of my efforts in regard to the text and "relating" Jesus' birth to that of "Ev'ry Child" came when I found—quite by accident—a wonderful quote by John Masefield (from The Everlasting Mercy) which says:
"And she who gives a baby birth
Brings Savior Christ again to earth."

That was a perfect "re-statement" of the same idea which I had had, and I sent the quote to Choristers Guild, hoping they would use it somehow on the cover, which they did. (The way I found the quote might also be of interest: my late husband, Ron, collected quotes in folders for possible use as sermon illustrations. After his death I was looking through certain ones of these and quite by chance came across the above quote. The marvelous thing was the timing of this discovery since it came just when I was completing the final writing of the anthem! I consider it a real gift, therefore, and was glad to have my thesis underlined by the well-known poet, John Masefield!)

111

Ev'ry Child

Ev'ry child is a gift of love
To the earth from Heaven sent down;
Filled with promises yet unknown
Like the babe of Bethl'hem town.

Ev'ry child is a sacred trust
Ever worthy in God's sight;
One small miracle here a while
Like the babe on Christmas night.

Let us welcome them now with joy
As we welcome the holy boy;
Guide them carefully so they know
Hope and happiness as they grow.

Ev'ry child brings us faith anew
In the wonder of it all:
God's continuing gifts of grace
Like the babe in Bethl'hem's stall . . .
God's continuing gifts of grace
Like the babe in Bethl'hem's man-ger stall.

O come, little children, O come, one and all,
To Bethlehem's stable, to Bethlehem's stall.
Rejoice, for the babe, who lies slumbering there,
Brings light and salvation, to babes ev'rywhere.

© 1986 by Choristers Guild.
Used by permission.

112

34. Hymn of Promise

This number was created almost immediately after "Happy Are They"* (Spring of '85), and I seem to have been much involved in pondering the ideas of life and death, spring and winter (which Denver weather was exhibiting about then on alternate days!), Good Friday and Easter, and the whole reawakening of the world that happens every spring. Some of it is related to the individual to whom "Happy Are They" is dedicated because he was facing an unbeatable battle with terminal cancer at the time, but there were also other "influences" which ultimately fed into this piece. The strange thing is that several of these factors seemed somehow to be connected to each other.

One evening we entertained a friend for supper and he, too, had been pondering such themes, and, even shared a work by T.S. Eliot in which there was a phrase something like "In our end is our beginning." That was virtually the catalyst for the form of the text of "Hymn of Promise" which I wrote in the next day or two. And this

*(AMSI)

friend *knew* Dale Tooley which was a further connection.

It also happened that there was scheduled a festival weekend and concert of my music at the Pasadena Community Church in St. Petersburg, Florida, in the middle of March, 1985. The director of the choirs there—Fred Harrison—had at one time in our planning expressed the hope that I might write a new anthem that they could premiere while we were down there, but I had not succeeded in doing that until this piece began to happen. As I pondered (and wrote) the text I thought that "Hymn of Promise" might *well* be appropriate to premiere in St. Petersburg, since it was almost officially spring then and since many of the members of the Pasadena Community Church are older people who might well be dealing with themes of "life and death and resurrection" (though *age* is not important in contemplating these matters!). So I sent Fred a copy of the manuscript about two weeks before we were due to come to St. Petersburg and the piece was, indeed, "premiered" on March 17th at the Natalie Sleeth concert there. I think at least 50 people must have come up to me and commented on the text especially; and when we got home, I heard from the publisher to whom I had sent the number saying that *he* thought it was one of the best texts I had ever written. So, I am glad the piece "happened" and that it apparently meant so much to those people in St. Petersburg as well as to the publisher and his editors. Hopefully it will reach out to many others and give them a lift as well.

I worked on the words very carefully, choosing just the right "pairings," attempting to get across the idea of something inherent in something else even though unseen, and I even bought a tulip plant (though it was in bloom and bright yellow) to contemplate the idea of the "bulb" leading to the flower even though the bulb itself seems "dead." Incidentally, the word *bulb* is very UNsingable and I usually try *not* to include such words in my texts. But it was also the only word that got the meaning I wanted across correctly, so I chose it and put a note in the song to sustain the vowel as long as possible which does the job. The rest of the words give no problem.

I once thought of entitling the piece "*Song* of Promise" but I already have a HOPE publication called "Song of Thanksgiving" and I didn't want to repeat myself. Also, *Hymn* suggests that perhaps a congregation could sing it and since it is basically a unison number (with Alleluia descant on the last verse) that is possible. In Florida, however, the choir sang it—Women on verse one, Men on verse two, and *all* singing melody on verse three except soprani who have the quiet descant. It worked well that way and because it is unison, the text [which, to me, is the essential part] comes out clearly.

. . . .

Epilogue

Soon after writing "Hymn of Promise," my husband became ill with what turned out to be a terminal malignancy. As the end neared he asked me to use "Hymn of Promise" as one of the anthems at his funeral service—which was done—and I subsequently (at publication) dedicated the piece to him. Again, a "mysterious" set of circumstances, but—perhaps again—a sort of "preparation."

115

Hymn of Promise

In the bulb, there is a flower;
In the seed, an apple tree;
In cocoons, a hidden promise:
Butterflies will soon be free!
In the cold and snow of winter
There's a Spring that waits to be,
Unrevealed until its season,
Something God alone can see.

There's a song in ev'ry silence,
Seeking word and melody;
There's a dawn in ev'ry darkness,
Bringing hope to you and me.
From the past will come the future;
What it holds, a mystery,
Unrevealed until its season,
Something God alone can see.

In our end is our beginning;
In our time, infinity.
In our doubt there is believing;
In our life, eternity.
In our death, a resurrection;
At the last, a victory,
Unrevealed until its season,
Something God alone can see.

Unrevealed until its season,
Something yet unknown,
Which God alone can see.

35. One Bright Candle

This piece came about because of the sad and premature death of a very special young girl from Manchester, Maine—Samantha Smith. I didn't of course know her personally but she had caught my attention because she wrote to the Russian premiere (who answered her letter) about world peace. A few years after that event she was co-starring with Robert Wagner in a new TV series (Lime Street) and after four episodes had been filmed in London she and her father were returning home to Maine when their plane crashed. I once heard Samantha interviewed on the Today Show, and she was such a sparkling, enthusiastic and sincere person (with no obvious egotism after what she had done), that she captured my heart as well as the hearts of all who watched her.

When she died so suddenly, I somehow wanted to write a piece that "highlighted" the idea that one person *can* make a difference—now and then, here and there— so that was the thesis behind "One Bright Candle." And, based on the example of one little girl, we can *all* try to do things that have the possibility of making a difference.

When I heard of Samantha's death, I wrote to her mother, Jane, and told her that I hoped to be able to write a piece that highlighted this theme. When I at last finished the piece, I sent her a copy of the text and said that I would send her copies of the published anthem when it was printed. In the meanwhile, a Samantha Smith Foundation was established which wrote to acknowledge my letters, and I sent them a donation with the promise that I would send copies of the piece when published. That I

117

did and I received a very gracious letter of thanks from Samantha's mother not long afterwards.

The piece is two-part, though it could be sung in unison, and is dedicated to Samantha.

One Bright Candle

One bright candle can light the dark,
One swift arrow can pierce the mark;
Make a diff'rence we can't deny;
So can you and I.

One small child can lead the way,
Bring us hope for a better day,
Have the courage to do or die,
So can you and I.

Who can number our length of days,
Be they great or few?
'Tis the way we would live that stays,
And the good we do.

One clear trumpet can sound the call,
One brave vision can start it all;
Change the future as time goes by,
So can you and I . . .

So can you . . .
So can I. . . .
If we dare to try! . . .

Copyright Owners Index

A.M.S.I., 2614 Nicollet Avenue, Minneapolis, MN 55408; (612) 872-8831.

BROADMAN PRESS, 127 Ninth Avenue North, Nashville, TN 37234; (616) 251-2000.

CARL FISCHER, INC., 62 Cooper Square, New York, NY 10003; (212) 777-0900.

CHORISTERS GUILD, 2834 W. Kingsley Rd., Garland, TX 75041; (214) 271-1521.

HINSHAW MUSIC, INC., P.O. Box 470, Chapel Hill, NC 27514; (919) 933-1691.

HOPE PUBLISHING COMPANY, Carol Stream, IL 60188; (312) 665-3200.

SACRED MUSIC PRESS, P.O. Box 802, Dayton, OH 45401; (513) 228-6118.

SONOS MUSIC RESOURCES, 1087 East 680 North, P.O. Box 1510, Orem, UT 84057 (801) 224-9933.

Natalie Sleeth's Published

TITLE	CODE NO
A Canon of Praise	A-79
A Little Love	HMI-340
• A Song of Thanksgiving	F 976
All Good Gifts	S-5784
Amen, So Be It	7807
Baby, What You Goin' To Be?	7790
	7791
Blessed Shall They Be	386
Blessing	A-145
Blessing II (on Back)	A-145
Bought With a Price	HMC-542
Bread and Wine	C-8
Calypso Christmas	A-508
Cantate (collection)	HMB-146

CONTENTS:

Cantate Domino	Behold the Shepherd
Comfort Ye	Let the Trumpet Sound
The Light Still Shines	Break the Bread

Carol of the Fisherman	249
• Christ Is Arisen, Indeed	A 527
Christmas Is a Feeling	HMC-116
Christmas Festival	HMC-587
• Come Before the Lord with Praise	F 975
Consider the Lilies	A-195
Deo Gracias	HMC-889

122

PUBLISHER	VOICING	CATEGORY	OPTIONS
Choristers Guild	3 pt. canon	general	bells
Hinshaw Music	1 or 2 pt.	general	
Hope Publishing Co.	SATB	Thanksgiving	trpt (2)
Sac. Mus./Lorenz	2 or 4 pt.	general	
Carl Fischer, Inc.	2 pt.	general	
Carl Fischer, Inc.	SATB vers.	Christmas	
Carl Fischer, Inc.	SA (Solo) vers.	Christmas	
AMSI	2 pt.	general	
Choristers Guild	Unison	general	fl/vln
Choristers Guild	Unison	(benediction)	
Hinshaw Music	2 pt.	general	
Choristers Guild	1, 2, and 3 pt.	Communion (8 sec)	
Hope Publishing Co.	SATB	Christmas	
Hinshaw Music	2 and 3 pts.	collection of 8	

For the Joy of Music
The Fruits of the Spirit

AMSI	1 or 2 pt.	general	
Hope Publishing Co.	SATB	Easter	
Hinshaw Music	1 or 2 pts.	Christmas	fl/vln
Hinshaw Music	SATB and Chil.	Christmas	inst.
Hope Publishing Co.	SATB	general	trpt (2)
Choristers Guild	Unison	general	fl/vln
Hinshaw Music	2 pt./Desc.	Christmas	

123

124

PUBLISHER	VOICING	CATEGORY	OPTIONS
Hinshaw Music	2 pt. vers.	general	
Hinshaw Music	4 pt. vers.	general	
Choristers Guild	Unis (A or Y)	Children Choir Christmas (general?)	
Choristers Guild	2 pt. (or 1 + fl)	general	
Carl Fischer, Inc.	SATB	general (sec)	
Carl Fischer, Inc.	Unison	general	fl (2)
Broadman Press	(2 or) 3 pt.	Lent	
AMSI	2 pt.	Christmas	trpt
Carl Fischer, Inc.	3 pt. Desc.	general	inst
Hinshaw Music, Inc.	2 pt.	Christmas	fl
Choristers Guild	Unison	gen. (Mother's Day)	
Carl Fischer, Inc.	Unison	general	
Choristers Guild	(2 or) 3 pt.	general	
Carl Fischer, Inc.	SATB	general (Sec)	
Sac. Mus./Lorenz	2 pt.	Christmas	
Hinshaw Music, Inc.	2 pt.	Easter	
AMSI	2 pt.	general (opt. cong)	
Carl Fischer, Inc.	Unison	general	fl
Choristers Guild	Unison	Palm Sunday	
Sonos Music Resourc.	SATB Solo/SA vers's.	general (esp. Mother's Day)	
Hope Publishing Co.	Unis/Desc.	general (Eas?)	
Fortress Press	(1), 2 & 3 parts	general (liturg)	
Sonos Music Resourc.	2 or 4 pt.	Patriotic	
Carl Fischer, Inc.	2 pt.	gen./Spring	

TITLE	CODE NO.
It's All in the Hands of God	421
Jazz Gloria	7752
Joy in the Morning	F 955
Jubilate Deo	AG 7257
Just Another Baby	4558-36
Laudamus (collection)	HMB-126

CONTENTS

Good News	It Is Good
Hodie	Laudamus Te
Hosanna	Look Down
If You Love Me	Only a Baby Came

Little By Little	HMC-126
Little Grey Donkey	A-84
Long Time Ago	S-5396
Lord Jesus, Be Near Me	7928
Lord, Make Us Worthy	276
Love Is a Song	HMC-186
Love One Another	A-480
Noel, Noel, a Boy Is Born	223
O Come, O Come, Immanuel	A-273
One Bright Candle	HMC-856
On Christmas Day	HMC-702
Psalm	441
Promised Land	S-5775
Sing the Lord's Song	HYM-625

PUBLISHER	VOICING	CATEGORY	OPTIONS
AMSI	2 pt.	general	
Carl Fischer, Inc.	SATB	Christmas	Inst
Hope Publishing Co.	SATB	general	trb/tr (2 ea.)
Hope Publishing Co. (orig. Abingdon)	Mult. Choirs	Easter	trb/tr (2 ea.)
Broadman Press	Unison	general (Lent?)	
Hinshaw Music, Inc.	1 and 2 pts.	collection (of 11)	

Seek and You Will Find
The Lord Be With You
With Music I Will Praise Thee

Hinshaw Music, Inc.	(1 or) 2 pts.	general	
Choristers Guild	Unison	Palm S.	Inst
Sac. Mus./Lorenz	2 pt.	general	
Carl Fischer, Inc.	Unison	general	Clar/Vcl
AMSI	2 pt.	general	
Hinshaw Music, Inc.	3 pt.	general	Pno. Duet/tr
Hope Publishing Co.	2 pt.	general	
AMSI	2 pt.	Christmas	bells
Choristers Guild	Unis./Desc.	Advent Christmas	
Hinshaw Music, Inc.	1 or 2 pt.	general	
Hinshaw Music, Inc.	2 pt.	Christmas	
AMSI	2 pt.	general	fl
Sac. Mus./Lorenz	2 pt.	general	
Hinshaw Music, Inc.	3 pt.	general	bells

127

TITLE	CODE NO.

Some Day Soon   7860
✓ – Spread Joy   7781
Sunday Songbook (collection)   HMB-102

CONTENTS:

Children of the Lord	Lullaby
For These Blessings	Part of the Plan
Go Now In Peace	Praise the Lord
Light One Candle	That's Good

The Kingdom of the Lord   301
The Lion and the Lamb   CGA-296
The Lord, He Made the Earth and Sky   232
The Lord Is My Shepherd   4560-93
The Time for Singing Has Come   S-285
There's Nothing Like a Song   HMC-459

They All Lived Long Ago   4558-24

This Land of Ours   7901
  (Band & cho. version also available)

Thy Church, O God   4551-04
Weekday Songbook (collection)   HMB-107

128

PUBLISHER	VOICING	CATEGORY	OPTIONS
Carl Fischer, Inc.	SATB (& Div)	general	
Carl Fischer, Inc.	3 pt.	general	tr
Hinshaw Music, Inc.	1 and 2 pt.	collection (of 12)	

The Holy Book
This Is the Day
Sing Noel
You and I

PUBLISHER	VOICING	CATEGORY	OPTIONS
AMSI	2 pt.	general	fl
Choristers Guild	Unison	general	
AMSI	2 pt.	general	
Broadman Press	Unis./Solo	general	
Sac. Mus./Lorenz	SATB	general (Sprg.)	
Hinshaw Music, Inc.	2 pt.	general	Pno. Duet
Broadman Press	Unison	general	(Opt. Ins)
Carl Fischer, Inc.	2 pt.	Patriotic	Pno. Duet & Inst.
Broadman Press	Unis./Desc	general	
Hinshaw Music	1 and 2 pts.	collection (of 12)	

TITLE   **CODE NO.**

CONTENTS:

130

PUBLISHER	VOICING	CATEGORY	OPTIONS
Try Again			
Two Roads			
We're On Our Way			
You Never Stop Learning			
AMSI	2 pt.	Lent	
Choristers Guild	Unison	Christmas	
Hope Publishing Co.	2 pt.	Christmas	
Carl Fischer, Inc.	SATB vers.	general	
Carl Fischer, Inc.	SA vers.	general	

Chronological Order (of the 35)

1972

 1. FEED MY LAMBS (Carl Fischer)
 2. SPREAD JOY (Carl Fischer)
 3. BABY, WHAT YOU GOIN' TO BE? (Carl Fischer)

1973

 4. GOD OF GREAT & GOD OF SMALL (Carl Fischer)

1974

 5. HAVE A GOOD DAY (Carl Fischer)

1975

 6. LORD, MAKE US WORTHY (AMSI)
 7. DOWN THE ROAD (Hinshaw Music)
 8. CHRISTMAS IS A FEELING (Hinshaw Music)

1976

 9. THE KINGDOM OF THE LORD (AMSI)
10. WERE YOU THERE ON THAT CHRISTMAS NIGHT?
    (Hope)
11. LOVE IS A SONG (Hinshaw Music)

1977

12. JOY IN THE MORNING (Hope)
13. KEEPING CHRISTMAS (WEEKDAY SONGBOOK
    —Hinshaw Music)

1978

14. CONSIDER THE LILIES (Choristers Guild)
15. A LITTLE LOVE (Hinshaw Music)

1979

16. PROMISED LAND (Sacred Music Press/Lorenz)
17. THE LORD IS MY SHEPHERD (Broadman Press)

1980

18. BLESSED SHALL THEY BE (AMSI)
19. THE LORD BE WITH YOU (LAUDAMUS—Hinshaw Music)
20. ONLY A BABY CAME (LAUDAMUS—Hinshaw Music)

1981

21. IT'S ALL IN THE HANDS OF GOD (AMSI)
22. BOUGHT WITH A PRICE (Hinshaw Music)

1982

23. O COME, O COME IMMANUEL (Choristers Guild)

1983

24. PSALM (AMSI)

1984

25. COMFORT YE (CANTATE—Hinshaw Music)
26. BEHOLD, THE SHEPHERD (CANTATE—Hinshaw Music)
27. BREAK THE BREAD (CANTATE—Hinshaw Music)
28. FOR THE JOY OF MUSIC (CANTATE—Hinshaw Music)
29. THE FRUITS OF THE SPIRIT (CANTATE—Hinshaw Music)

1985

30. HAPPY ARE THEY (AMSI)
31. ALL GOOD GIFTS (Sacred Music Press/Lorenz)
32. HOW WILL THEY KNOW? (Sonos Music Resources)

1986

33. EV'RY CHILD (Choristers Guild)
34. HYMN OF PROMISE (Hope)
35. ONE BRIGHT CANDLE (Hinshaw Music)

134

Index for the Church Year

135

136

COMMUNION

Alphabetical Index (of the 35)

138

✓ P. 28 Spread Joy Fischer ✓

✓ P. 76 st'd All in the Hands of God ✓ AMSI

✓ P. 79 Bought with a price Hinshaw Lent

✓ P. 85 Psalm AMSI ✓ — all others
✓ 98 Happy are they AMSI ✓ " general "

✓ 162 All Good Gifts Lorenz ✓

I Sing of America (Sonos)

___ = rec'd.